Letting Go of Our Adult Children

Letting Go
of Our Adult
Children
When
what we do
is never
enough

ARLENE HARDER, M.F.C.C.

BOB ADAMS, INC.
Holbrook, Massachusetts

Published by Bob Adams, Inc., 260 Center Street, Holbrook, MA 02343

ISBN: 1-55850-289-0

Printed in the United States of America

A   B   C   D   E   F   G   H   I   J

Library of Congress Cataloging-in-Publication Data
Harder, Arlene.
  Letting go of our adult children : when what we do is never enough / Arlene Harder.
    p.   cm.
  Includes index.
  ISBN 1-55850-289-0 : $7.95
  1. Parent and adult child—United States. 2. Intergenerational relations—United States.
  I. Title.
  HQ755.86.H37 1994
  306.874—dc20   93-32455
                                                                        CIP

This book is available at quantity discounts for bulk purchases.
For information, call 1-800-872-5627.

Grateful acknowledgment is made to the following individuals and organizations who provided the author with permission to quote from their work.
The excerpt from Suzanne Gordon's column that appears on page 52-53 is used by permission. Copyright (c) 1993 Suzanne Gordon. All rights reserved. The excerpt on pages 75-76 is reprinted by permission of Warner Books/New York from *Once My Child . . . Now My Friend*. Copyright (c) 1981 by Elinor Lenz. All rights reserved. The excerpt on pages 96 is reprinted by permission of HarperCollins Publishers, Inc. from *The Hero Within*. Copyright (c)1987 by Carol S. Pearson. All rights reserved. The excerpt on page 108 is reprinted by permission of Ann Landers and Creators Syndicate. All rights reserved. The excerpt on pages 112-113 is reprinted by permission of Warner Books/New York from *Guilt is the Teacher, Love is the Lesson*. Copyright (c) 1990 Joan Borysenko. All rights reserved. The excerpt on page 120 is from Lance Morrow's article in the October 28, 1991 issue of TIME Magazine, "Truth in the Ruins." Copyright (c) 1991, Time Inc. Reprinted by permission. All rights reserved. The excerpt on page 127 is by Mary Jo Barrett and Terry S. Trooper, and is from the May/June, 1992 issue of *The Family Therapy Networker*. Reprinted with permission of *The Family Therapy Networker*. All rights reserved. The poem "An Autobiography in Five Short Chapters" by Portia Nelson first appeared in Claudia Black's book, *Repeat After Me*. Reprinted with permission by Claudja, Inc. All rights reserved. The quotes from Patty McConnell that appear on page 148 are reprinted by permission of HarperCollins Publishers from her book *A Workbook for Healing*. Copyright (c) 1986 by Harper & Row, Publishers, Inc. This material also appeared in an adapted version in the publication *Mothering*, and is excerpted with permission from Volume 46 of *Mothering*, P.O. Box 1690, Santa Fe NM 87504. Back issues of *Mothering* are available at $4.00 each, and special publications on vaccination and circumcision are available by writing to the Santa Fe address. All rights reserved. The forgiveness techniques reproduced on page 150 are reprinted by permission of HarperCollins Publishers from Patty McConnell's book *A Workbook for Healing*. Copyright (c) 1986 by Harper & Row, Publishers, Inc. All rights reserved. The text that appears on page 168 is reprinted with the kind permission of Grace Walls. All rights reserved. The piece "What I Learned in Fifty Years" by Gary Docherty that appears on pp. 187-188 is reprinted with the kind permission of Gary Docherty. All rights reserved.

This book is dedicated to all parents
who are learning to let go of their adult children—
especially when their children have not turned out
the way the parents expected and have chosen
to live by different values and lifestyles.

Contents

Acknowledgments

This book is possible because I was helped by many people as I struggled toward letting go of an adult child who did not meet the expectations I had for him. Through their support I was able to finally achieve peace and later to help others understand the stages of healing I had gone through. Writing about my own journey and that of my clients has been an exciting challenge and there are many who deserve special recognition, especially: my family for their support even though we differed in our approaches to healing; my friend Lynn Bellinger for helping me ride our emotional roller coaster by listening to the trials of our family and being there when I needed her; my therapist Chris Varnes for the many times she helped me see through new windows and for her encouragement in putting my experience on paper; my clients for teaching me by their willingness to change their focus from problems of their adult children to their own issues; the many parents I interviewed, both those satisfied and those dissatisfied with how their children turned out, for adding their stories and perspectives on how to allow grown children to live independent lives; my friend Janet Rouse for her many suggestions and support in putting my initial ideas on paper; my agents Rosalie and Jim Heacock and my publisher Bob Adams for recognizing the need for this book; my friend Miles Clark whose editorial comments kept me focused on the direction that could best help the reader; my colleagues and friends Diana Dial, Ivajoy Draper, Gabrilla Hoeglund, Laura Kluter, and Jan Kuzmic for reading the manuscript.

Introduction

Letting go of adult children. It's something parents do all the time. At least we're told that's what parents are *supposed* to do about the time their children turn eighteen. Whether our children stay under our roof longer than we want or strike out earlier than anticipated, we are told we need to cut the apron strings that have kept us focused on our child.

In other words, when our children reach the age of maturity, we are expected to make a major change in our relationship with them—to transfer responsibility for decisions concerning their lives from *us* to *them*. If we successfully complete this transition, we will, says conventional wisdom, accept our children as independent individuals just as they are, including imperfections, values that conflict with ours, and different needs and desires. And they will accept us in return. We will communicate openly and share our values and experiences with one another without believing we have the right, or the power, to change the other person.

Sound easy? Not if you're the parent of a grown child who marches to a drum very different from the one you played for your child when he or she was young. You know it would be better for both of you if you could let go. But you can't. You remain uncomfortably, perhaps painfully, "stuck" because things haven't turned out the way you expected.

Being stuck and unable to let go can arise from minor, irritating differences between you and your child or major obstacles that appear to be intractable.

For example, you may be unable to get past frequent arguments over relatively unimportant issues that both of you always seem to turn into contests of who is right. Or while you and your daughter don't often disagree, you can't shake the disappointment you feel when she loses yet another job. You *want* to accept the fact that how well she does at work is *her* problem. But you know she doesn't demonstrate the commitment to work that employers want. How can you let go when you blame yourself for not teaching her responsibility? Or perhaps you need the money from the sale of a family house your thirty-eight year old son has been living in rent-free for fifteen years. The only "problem" is that he doesn't have money to move elsewhere; forcing him out would make you feel like Simon Legree. Or while you may realize that there is probably nothing you can do to prevent your son's divorce, you remain entangled in accusations and defenses with your son's in-laws because you're afraid you will lose contact with a precious grandchild. And sticky in-law problems are legion in complicated stepfamily configurations.

Even if your children are happily married, however, you may have a hard time understanding and accepting in-laws who are of a different race, religion, or social group. You hadn't thought of yourself as prejudiced, but you are having a hard time adjusting. And what if your child is single and living with a member of the opposite sex—or has chosen a member of his or her same sex as a life partner? With less than 25 percent of families made up of father, mother, and dependent children, family constellations aren't what they used to be.

Letting go may be particularly difficult if the problems you face seem highly resistant to change. This is especially true when your child is mentally ill or is in serious trouble with the law. And if your child is like my son, whose difficulties in relationships and jobs have been compounded by drug and alcohol abuse, the road to letting go can be extremely long and trying. Yet your situation may be even *more* painful if your child died before you were able to work out the issues that kept you from letting go; all that unfinished business leaves you with pain you are sure will never go away.

You may be a parent who claims *you have no choice* but to let go when your child refuses to have any contact, or has extremely minimal contact, with you. Don't kid yourself. On the surface you may *look* as though you have let go, but anyone probing a centimeter deep can see that your hurt in being excluded from your child's life penetrates deep into your heart. This may be especially difficult if you are at a loss to understand what went wrong.

Yet the situation isn't any easier if you recognize all too clearly how you contributed to the rift that has torn the family fabric in half. For example, perhaps you abused alcohol or drugs when your children were small. Today, although you are now clean and sober, your child is unwilling to forgive you, despite your apologies. In that case you may be paralyzed by guilt—concluding that you have permanently injured your child and that the gap between you can never be bridged.

On the other hand, you may be a parent who is perfectly satisfied with how your child has turned out and who thought you had a good relationship with her. Recently, however, she has accused you and her father of being "dysfunctional" and perhaps even "abusive." Even though you realize you weren't perfect parents, you are saddened by alienation created by her anger and your hurt.

If you see yourself in any of these situations (or ones uncomfortably similar), you realize that you've been unable to let go no matter how hard you try. This is what is meant by the subtitle of this book, "When What We Do Is Never Enough." No matter what we say, think or do—no matter how hard we try—until we let go with love we remain uncomfortably bound to a child who is legally old enough to make his decisions without parental interference or approval.

As parents of children whose values and lifestyles are in conflict with ours—whether we experience a fairly small amount or a great deal of disappointment in that fact—we have probably already discovered that heavy-handed bullying and significant bribes cannot make our child become what we had hoped he would become. Money may work in the short run, of course, but in the long haul it can't buy the integrity, honesty, determination, and responsibility we desire for our child. Yet masking our attempts to change our child through less obvious measures is not unlike trying to run him over with a fuzzy bulldozer; it only leaves him, and us, bruised. Let's face it—as long as we keep trying to get our child to live according to *our* values, we don't stand much chance of having the kind of adult-to-adult relationship we all deserve with our children when they grow up.

The first part of the book, "Getting Caught up in Our Expectations," deals with what happens when parents discover their child is marching to a different drummer. In it I offer a path to letting go with love and to forming a more positive relationship with your adult child, a path involving five stages of healing. In these chapters you will see that your disappointment and pain are not unique; nor is it unusual for you to keep trying to get your child to change. Most important of all, you will realize why it is essential for you to shift your attention from your adult child to yourself.

If you already know you must change your focus away from whatever stands between you and your child, you may want to go directly to the second part of the book, "Finding Peace by Letting Go." These five chapters offer suggestions for healing the pain caused by the realization that your child does not share your values or cannot live up to the expectations you once had for him or her. Here you will find motivation to explore the issues that keep you pulling on your end of the rope in the family tug-of-war, to grieve your unfulfilled expectations, to forgive yourself and your child and, finally, to let go with love. And if differences between you and your child are still irreconcilable, you can learn how to bring closure and healing to that situation as well.

The concept of a path of healing for parents first arose for me during the painful years when I struggled with great disappointment in a child who was not living the kind of life I envisioned for him. Gradually I realized that I was moving through a series of stages and turned my attention from my son's problems to those which I needed to address in my own life. I continued to observe this process and to further develop my theory in working with disappointed parents as part of my practice as a licensed family therapist. Later these ideas were reinforced in interviews with over seventy-five parents, both those who were disappointed in how things have turned out and those who were very satisfied.

To protect confidentiality in sharing the stories of others, I have changed names and identifying characteristics. In a few instances I have combined several elements from more than one situation to emphasize a particular point.

Letting go can be difficult for parents whether they are married, divorced, or widowed; adoptive or biological parents; single or stepparents. Since the specific circumstances in everyone's life are different, and since we all have somewhat different expectations for our children, we will each experience different reactions to our adult children if those expectations are not met. Consequently, the act of letting go with love will be easier and go more quickly for some and be more difficult and take longer for others. Yet this book offers to every parent the evidence that *it is possible to let go and find peace even in the most difficult of circumstances.*

A brief word about the use of pronouns in the text. The title of this book contains the words "our children" because I have walked the same path to letting go that the reader is also walking. And because this book is a road map based in large part on my personal and professional experience, I also use the words "me," "mine," "us," and "ours." I probably have experienced many of your struggles, and I believe we can more easily learn to let go when we see that our problems do not fall only on our shoulders but are shared by millions of others.

I have generally found that mothers experience more guilt than fathers over a child who hasn't met the family's expectations or lived up to family values. Fathers can also have a difficult time in letting go of their adult children, but they have not been conditioned to feel as *personally* responsible as do their wives. Therefore, in an attempt to avoid the him-or-her, his-or-hers dilemma, I use "she" more frequently than "he" when I refer to an individual parent. In discussing children, however, I have attempted to use "he" and "she" in equal amounts. I don't want to create the impression that only male children are embroiled in the kinds of generation gaps that pull families apart.

It is my hope that this book will guide you in moving past your disappointment and pain into peace, healing, and acceptance of your child, even if he or she continues to make choices that have, until now, driven you up a wall.

We cannot change our grown children. But dealing honestly and openly with our disappointment creates an opportunity to change ourselves—and in the process to let go with love so that our disappointment no longer causes us pain.

PART ONE

Getting Caught up in Our Expectations

Chapter 1

Something Unexpected Happened on the Way to My Ideal Family

Four hours after our first child was born, Bob wrote me a letter in red pencil. He said that day was his "red letter day" because I had given him a beautiful daughter, the beginning of what was sure to be a fine family. The letter is a special treasure, for it highlighted my awareness that, finally, I was a mother, my "proper role" in life. When our children were grown, successful and independent, I would look back with pleasure and pride at how well I had done the job of mothering. Success was surely programmed into my DNA.

This rosy picture of the future was part and parcel of every family magazine in the thirties, forties, and fifties; it was also painted with broad strokes in middle-class homes across America. From the time I was a small girl my parents had told me I would get married and have a family, just as my grandparents and great-grandparents had been doing successfully for generations. Pictures in family albums and visits with aunts, uncles, and cousins convinced me that parental success was woven into the fabric of our family.

Had I paid greater attention, I would have noticed that not all my relatives were perfectly happy. One of my cousins had been married three times and was estranged from her family. Another cousin had divorced twice. Another left her husband when her children were very little and did not reconcile with him until many years later. My father's mother committed suicide (although for many years we were told she died of cancer). But to the extent these situations were acknowledged, they were considered aberrations. In any case, I knew that *I* would parent the *right* way. Our children would be protected from the frailties and pitfalls that sidetrack others.

I was in for a rude awakening.

A Train Derailed

Three of our children turned out more or less as I expected. For example, they have all graduated with honors from college: Diane, now 32, in Latin American studies, Rebecca, 28, in history, and Brad, her twin, in elementary education. Honors were not expected of them, even though they are all gifted. But we did assume they would finish college, unless they had shown an aptitude in a field that did not require higher education. Our ideas of "successful" careers didn't focus on having them strive to become president of the United States, CEO of a major company, winner of the Nobel prize in literature, or any other position that would demonstrate they were the *best* in their field. Doing honest work they enjoyed was all we expected. Today Diane is happily pursuing a career in computer programming after spending several years working in fund raising for non-profit organizations. Rebecca plans to enter graduate school in the field of geography, and Brad will get his teaching certificate next year.

All of our children are individualists.

Diane is an extrovert who is very interested in observing how people's temperaments fit certain profiles. She likes dancing, hiking, camping, church activities, and family reunions. As a teenager she was fascinated by geneaology, even that of acquaintances, and she has now become the family record keeper of marriages, births, and deaths for aunts and uncles, cousins and second cousins once removed.

Rebecca is quite different from her sister and has many interests and talents, which include traveling, feminist issues, reading, bike riding, hiking, and piano playing. Although more introverted than her sister, one summer she spent three months in Europe meeting new people and having a wonderful time; after graduation from college she traveled for three months across the United States and is working to save enough money to leave California for new adventures elsewhere.

Brad is laid-back and fairly easygoing. After high school he took a job as a tow truck operator, and during college worked as a caretaker of disabled children and young adults. He backpacks, rides a mountain bike, plays the guitar in a small band, and is a creative and talented potter.

We see Diane, Rebecca and Brad as often as possible, and our relationships with them are growing more satisfying all the time as we learn what it means to be parents of adult children actively pursuing lives of their own. As I said, they are individualists. None of them, however, is an individualist quite like our second child, David, now thirty-one.

To begin with, although he is gifted like the others, he has had almost no college experience. And while sharing some of the enthusiasm for life which his siblings exhibit, the story of where he is heading (at least up to this point) is very, very different from the direction they are traveling.

Our view of David as "different" is not because he advocates macrobiotic food, doesn't want to live anywhere near a city, writes original music, and plays the guitar. Nor is he different just because he lives with the mother of his child, our first grandchild, and her two other sons on a piece of land without running water or electricity two miles from a paved road.

His lifestyle choices are foreign to us because he is not willing to work (claiming he can't work for anyone who isn't as smart as he is, although he's worked in the past) and because his finances come from Social Security Disability. He draws this government support because of what he claims is "mental instability" created by drugs and alcohol. His personality certainly has been affected in some ways by past abuse, although he does not appear to us to have been damaged enough to prevent him from pursuing gainful employment. Nevertheless, for several years he lived on the streets in northern California. And while he claims to be completely satisfied with his lifestyle, clearly his future is not likely to fulfill the dreams we had for him.

Somehow my husband and I were not able to assure our son a life either drug-free or successful by middle-class standards. So the train of parenting I entered with confidence and enthusiasm got derailed somewhere along the way.

Hanging on our wall is a collage of family photos, including one of David when he was ten. With hands on his hips he stands proudly in front of a mariposa pine in Yosemite, grinning from ear to ear. This is the picture of a child we expected, when he was young, to make a significant difference in the world through his talents and many interests. He had the creative capacity to design a building that conserved energy more efficiently, to write a prize-winning play, to build the proverbial better mouse trap.

When I reflect upon the potential that picture represents and compare it with the path my son has chosen, tears sometimes come to my eyes. Yet the picture stays on the wall to remind me of the good times we have had. I welcome my tears because they help wash away the pain of disappointment and lost dreams. Grieving must come before letting go.

What Kind of Home Did We Create for Our Children?

What happened to the good intentions we experienced on that red-letter day our parenting began? What caused our train to end up so far from our original destination? Our dreams were no different than those of countless parents who have high hopes for their families. Why weren't we successful while other families were? I needed answers to these questions if I was to understand and heal my pain and disappointment.

Since David's experimental use of marijuana in high school created the most noticeable change in him, and in our family, I began looking for answers by exploring what happened at that point in time. How did he develop the pattern of chemical use, and then abuse, that affected almost every aspect of his life? I knew that David did not look on Bob and me as models for his behavior, as we are extremely moderate drinkers and don't use any mood-altering drugs, illegal or otherwise. Of course, alcohol and marijuana were all too easily available from friends and others, as many parents have unhappily discovered. Yet blaming "society" seemed too pat an explanation for what went wrong. However, satisfactory answers *might* come by looking further back into our family's past. I would need to do some serious sleuthing if I were to uncover more than a superficial answer.

Although exploring the environment in our home meant I would probably need to confront mistakes I might be embarrassed to admit, the pain of my estrangement from our son overshadowed any reluctance to dig into the past. If digging could help me make sense of what happened, I was willing to dig.

No analysis—least of all the biased analysis of a family member—can accurately describe the innumerable characteristics that make up a family. More than that, the hundreds of experiences, qualities, and traits of each person, positive and negative, are synergistic, creating a whole picture much different from what the separate pieces might suggest when viewed separately. And so I am aware that any evaluation of myself and my family must be not only biased but also incomplete, even if space did not preclude a more detailed story. Nevertheless, the limited portrait I present here is as honest as I can make it.

Bedtime Stories and Other Good Stuff

A lot of water has flowed under the bridge since I first became a mother. And if I had to do it over again, I would be a very different kind of parent. Yet despite the many lessons I needed to learn, I believe that basically our children had a good start in life.

I rocked them, nursed them, hugged them, read to them and told them I loved them. As we worked together to assemble puzzles, construct block houses, and play hundreds of games, I knew mothering was a job I would always love—and couldn't imagine our children would be hard to handle when they became teenagers.

There were picnics in local parks and in the mountains above our home; trips to the zoo and the beach; camping vacations. We hiked because Bob and I liked the outdoors, and our children learned to enjoy it as well.

There were swimming lessons, piano lessons, art classes, karate lessons, Cub Scouts, Brownies, and marching with the Indian Maidens in our community's Old-Fashioned Days parade.

Since we were in California, isolated from the rest of the family who lived primarily in Ohio and Pennsylvania, we wanted our children to know they were part of a wider family unit. So we periodically took trips back East for family reunions, and the grandparents came to visit every year or so. Considering the distance, our children got to know their cousins as well as could be expected.

As I review the many positive things we did for our children, there was one that seems to me most important. Our children had the security of knowing their parents loved and respected each other. While there are *many* differences between my husband and me, we both came from homes where divorce was seldom considered. Consequently, we worked (and stumbled) through a number of our problems. In the process, we also papered over other issues that should have been addressed.

A Perfectionist Mother Trying to Do Things Right

When I began motherhood, I was fairly liberal politically but fairly rigid in how I viewed my role as parent. This was partly the result of my temperament and partly the consequence of a childhood in which there were many "shoulds," "oughts," "rights," and "wrongs." Although I didn't insist on spotless floors and neatly made beds, being a perfectionist permeated many facets of my parenting.

As a child I never questioned whether I was being asked to be perfect; my siblings were also perfectionists in one way or another. Our parents' high standards left little room to question the reasons for their rules and values—an attitude typical for that generation. When a child was told to jump, she was expected to say, "How high?" and not, "Why?"

As a recovering perfectionist I can see why perfectionism is a common feature of the human character. After all, perfectionists give the best they have to offer. You can generally count on them to do what they say they'll do, even if it means giving up their own needs to be sure you're satisfied. On the other hand, I now realize that the standards of perfectionists are usually those others consider "right," not necessarily those the perfectionist herself would choose—if she could freely follow the dictates of her own heart.

It is this last characteristic of perfectionism that gave me the most trouble. I was so busy trying to discover what others said was "right" that I neglected to listen to my own heart. At the time, however, I was too unsure of myself even to know such an option existed.

As the years progressed, however, I suspected something was amiss in the way I viewed parenting—and life in general. Other parents seemed to expend a lot less energy and have more fun in the process. I also noticed that their children usually seemed to be doing just fine. So with determination I set about changing myself. Yet major personality changes aren't made overnight. By the time I had become more relaxed, less of a perfectionist, and less controlling, my children were well on their way to becoming young adults.

A Gentle and Quiet Father with a Laissez-faire Attitude

My aunt said my husband was "a very special ordinary man." I would add that he is a "self-contained man," reserved, generous, conservative, a lover of puns and honest as the day is long. Bob doesn't like pretensions and prefers function over style (he would never win a fashion contest). At home he has often been a Mr. Fixit for cars and broken appliances and a reluctant mower of lawns. At work he is very conscientious as a computer expert in the analysis of stress on materials.

Unlike me, Bob does not express much outward curiosity or interest in why other people live the way they do. He views the world primarily through his own experiences. It is this characteristic, I believe, together with his reluctance to express emotions openly—the buried-feelings syndrome common among men of his generation—that sometimes made it difficult for him to understand his children and to relate more intimately with them.

Bob did very well in school without any pressure to achieve and did not believe it necessary to demand that his children had to make high grades. He believed they would do fine if we left them alone. Since he hadn't rebelled against his parents, it was beyond his comprehension when David rebelled against our values or experimented with drugs. Bob had given up smoking cold turkey, and assumed that anyone could stop abusing drugs simply by using will power.

Inconsistent Discipline

Bob's main role in disciplining our children was getting them to do jobs in the front and back yards once a week. His approach was usually to tell them what he expected them to do, seldom allowing discussion or negotiation.

On the other hand, as the parent at home all day (until the twins were thirteen and I went back to work), I found myself responsible for the children's daily chores, for overseeing their squabbles, keeping an eye open for mischief, and taking note of problems with school and playmates. Unwittingly I became the "heavy," a mother who dominated many parenting decisions and resented her role—but didn't know how to get out of it. Even family meetings, which I called in the hope of getting off the hot seat, were seldom successful in shifting responsibility off my shoulders.

Discovering an effective method of discipline took longer than the time I had to raise our children. Today I know what would have worked. Then I didn't. All I knew was that I didn't want to use spanking or because-I-told-you-so rules, as my parents had done. To find an approach that was more gentle, but firm, I tried every method offered by parenting magazines and swung from one to the other like a pendulum.

First I would be too permissive and our children could easily manipulate me. For example, since I resented it when as a child my father wouldn't explain the reasons for his rules, I decided to explain things to my children. The result was that it sometimes required forty-five minutes to discuss with a child why he or she had to do a five minute task!

When it was clear that our children needed more direction and control, I made lots of rules and backed them up with what I considered "consequences" (our children called them "punishments"). Whatever they were called, my follow-through was often poor. And when my stricter approach didn't work well, I reverted back to a more permissive style. Inconsistency was my most outstanding and self-defeating trait. Our children learned to tolerate any kind of discipline because they knew it would change when I tried something else.

Self-esteem Building Needed a Boost

"Self-esteem" is a word that describes an essential ingredient for a healthy life. Developing this trait of self-worth in our children wasn't our strongest suit.

As a child I thought I had to *do* something to merit my parent's affection. I still have great difficulty in just *being* rather than in *doing*. It is not surprising that I wasn't good at showing my children that they didn't need to earn my love, even though I felt that way.

Bob, too, clearly loved his children, was proud of their accomplishments and tried to support them in the ways he knew how. Yet he did not dispense ego-boosting compliments easily (although lately he has gotten better in that regard). He was not aware that children need to have their accomplishments acknowledged and to hear their parents frequently say "I love you." But words were not his medium and he wasn't big on hugging.

Another self-esteem issue that grew out of Bob's more quiet manner concerns the difficulty he often had in saying, "I'm sorry" or "I made a mistake," even when he knew he was wrong. I believe this is because his father, like mine, almost never apologized. Yet self-esteem develops, in part, when children can see that people, including parents, are not diminished in stature when they have made a mistake, admit it, and learn from it.

Manners Left on the Doorstep

Bob and I treat each other kindly even when we disagree. Yet sometimes our children fought and were quite disrespectful toward each other. For a long time I wondered why.

Then a couple years ago I read an article by Miss Manners that expressed our situation perfectly. She spoke about the attitude of insisting on one's right to "be myself" and how that affects others. I had been determined to let my children "be themselves" in their own home, since as a child I did not feel I was allowed to be *just plain me*. While our children weren't permitted to be truly barbarians toward each other, they were given permission to express their disagreeableness in ways I would not tolerate today. Too often we allowed them to leave their manners on the doorstep when they entered the house.

Had we insisted on consideration of others' needs and on better manners, David could not have bullied the others when he became a teenager. He might also have received from them the respect he needed to build his self-esteem.

Ineffective Problem Solving Widens the Gulf

To solve the many problems that arise in any family, parents need an effective method of conflict resolution. Unfortunately, neither of us brought to our marriage the skills needed for healthy disagreement between spouses.

Before my parents had children, they made a pact in which my mother agreed not to disagree with my father in front of us. Consequently, for many years, whenever Bob and I did not see eye to eye, I feared that our disagreements might invalidate our love. So instead of openly addressing issues, I often used subtle manipulation to get my way. But Bob also had no opportunity to learn give-and-take skills of conflict resolution because his father, who was the dominant parent in much the same way as mine, didn't discuss matters openly either. It has only been in recent years that we have developed the ability to resolve our differences more easily.

Unfortunately, there was one dynamic in communication between Bob and me during our child rearing years that was more serious than our inability to reach a consensus openly and directly. We often *avoided* dealing with our conflicts altogether by focusing on what David was doing. When he was little we labeled him as the child who "got into trouble," although I now believe that label had less to do with his behavior than with our ineffective discipline. David almost always tried to see how much he could get away with. His mischief kept us on our toes. In any case, by focusing on our son, Bob and I unconsciously used him to avoid important issues between us that should have been addressed. When Bob got home from work, it was much easier to say, "Let me tell you what David did today," rather than, "Something is bothering me about us."

A Hippopotamus in Our Living Room

When our train came around the teenage bend, our family might still have come through fairly unscathed, even though the ride had become a little bumpy. Despite our imperfections we were a fairly typical family. Many families just like ours have been successful in achieving their goals. But when we came upon marijuana and other drugs scattered across our tracks, we were unprepared for this new and difficult challenge.

As with almost all families dealing with drug and/or alcohol problems, it was a long time before we would admit that we had a serious problem and that everyone in the family was affected by it. A popular analogy is that families like ours *have a hippopotamus in the living room, but the family pretends it isn't there.* Other people know this animal is tearing up the fabric of the family; the family either can't see it or is afraid to acknowledge its existence.

We clearly needed help to deal with the strange animal in our midst.

David's drug use required strong, united action on our part. Yet Bob denied there was a problem long after it was obvious to me and to others outside the family. I was too unsure of myself to take a unilateral position to force our son into therapy or treatment, although I certainly solicited a ton of advice from friends and experts. During part of this time I was even working at a drug counseling center for teenagers! The result of my efforts was to try a variety of approaches, from ignoring the growing problem ("it's only a phase") to variations on the theme of Tough Love, a philosophy that encourages parents to set and carry through on firm, consistent limits.

It was not our fault that our son chose to use drugs! But if we had gotten our parent act together before his teen years started, we might have addressed the problem with the cooperation that was needed once it began.

When the hippopotamus took over, our family was affected in at least three important ways as David's drug use gradually became more serious.

The first occurred because we responded to David with extra (albeit often negative) attention. Naturally his siblings resented this, but we were too absorbed in trying to handle *his* situation to respond effectively to *their* needs. Furthermore, for many years I had assumed David's getting into "trouble" meant he *needed* special attention from us. When he started using marijuana, I was convinced that he wouldn't need drugs to feel better if I could just get him to see that we really loved him.

Unwittingly we created, I believe, a situation in which our disproportionate attention contributed to his sense of entitlement, a trait many addicts share. For example, addicts frequently want others to make exceptions for them. They think they should be excused for returning late from lunch, for not handing in a term paper on time, for not paying rent when it's due. If caught driving under the influence, their greatest anger is often directed not against themselves for endangering the lives of others (which might mean they would not do it again) but against their dumb luck for getting caught or against the police officer who arrested them.

The second way our family was affected by David's use of drugs and alcohol was by the constant adjustment of our lives to fit his unpredictable moods—moods that changed depending upon whether he was using marijuana, something else, or no drugs at all. I was the mother of a feisty lion cub one day and a sweet lamb the next. It was as though we were being forced to ride his roller coaster until he decided to stop.

The third area in which our son's drug use affected us was a cycle of hope and despair that drove me crazy and contributed to my inability to take more decisive action. When David made a promise to stop using, I would desperately hope that *this* time, finally, he meant what he said and our family could get back on a steadier course. But he was unable to keep his promises, and my hopes would crash once more. Twice I asked him to move out of our house and twice, after a period of several months during which time we had settled into a calmer home atmosphere, he would ask to return, promising things would be better. Wanting to believe him, we accepted him back. Only much later did I realize that the seductive power of drugs is so powerful that it can overcome the most honest intention in the world. Promises are easy. Giving up drugs is not.

I had the illusion that if I could only "reason" with him he would see how his drug use was affecting school and jobs, to say nothing of relationships with friends and family. It took me a *very* long time to realize that it was useless to attempt communicating with our son when he had drugs in his system. Until his drug use could be stopped, we were talking to the drug that possessed his body, not with the person who was using the drug.

In 1984 Bob and I returned from a long vacation to find David convinced he would receive the Nobel prize for physics because of insights he received under the influence of LSD. An attempt to have him enter a treatment program was unsuccessful. So two weeks after his twenty-second birthday, David was asked to leave home for what would be the last time. Although it was the best decision we could have made, that was the most difficult and painful day in our lives.

Our Family's Pain Slowly Heals

Since that terrible day, each of the members in our family has struggled to come to terms with this major rupture in our lives. Unfortunately, we did not have an effective mechanism with which we could support each other and receive healing within the family itself.

As a mother who bought the myth that I could have prevented the rift in my family if only I had been a "better" parent, I was wrenched by guilt. Furthermore, in my perfectionistic, self-judging style, I jumped to the conclusion that Bob held me responsible for how things had turned out. That seemed especially unfair because I had tried and tried and tried to be the best mother I could be. If nothing more, I desperately wanted Bob to acknowledge how much I had tried.

But Bob approached parenting as something he did the best way he knew how; he is not introspective by nature and doesn't analyze what he "might have done better." Once our problems with David were out of our hands and Bob knew we couldn't do anything more about them, he saw no use in dwelling on the past or on our role as parents.

Eventually I shifted from a focus on my "failure" as a parent to grief that the hopes and dreams we had for our son would not be fulfilled. I could see there was absolutely nothing we could *do* to bring David back into the family whole and well again. We could only wait and hope. Yet I wanted Bob's consolation, his assurance that he understood my grief. Again, because of who he was, that was not easy for him to do. I felt alone with my pain. Bob seemed to handle his by burying it somewhere deep inside.

Fortunately there were sources of comfort for me outside my family. My good friend Lynn Bellinger listened to my frequent strategies for change, my hope when promises were made, and my pain when things did not change. She knew all about our roller-coaster ride and provided the support and loving care I needed desperately, for which I will always be grateful. Most of my colleagues also understood my pain and offered their support in various ways. All of this was invaluable. But my greatest movement toward healing the pain in my heart came through work with a therapist who helped me shift my focus from what I *could not do* to get David to change to what I *could do* to change myself.

For the most part our daughter Diane has seemed to work through some of her issues with David by talking with friends whose siblings had similar problems. I am glad she had others to whom she could turn, for I was not a good source of support. For many years my own pain got in the way as I sometimes defended my actions when I should have simply accepted her need to be angry that Bob and I didn't handle the drug problem better.

When Brad moved to northern California to attend college, David, who had recently lost another job, soon followed. Brad generally accepted David just as he was, and at first things were okay between them. Soon, however, there were altercations, and their relationship was painfully severed. We lived too far away to support Brad adequately as he struggled with David's erratic and irrational behavior. In recent years, as David has become more mellow and less volatile, he sometimes goes to Brad's place to play guitar, as they had done together in the past. What the future will hold for their friendship remains uncertain.

Rebecca felt particularly cheated because staying *out* of trouble couldn't capture her parents' attention nearly as easily as David's getting *into* trouble did. Both because of her own coping style and because David could be verbally abusive to her (especially when we weren't home to stop him), her reaction has been to distance herself from him emotionally. Today she accepts him fairly matter-of-factly as a person who may need care, but not as one who is connected with her in any significant way.

Finally Letting Go with Love

Three years ago, on one of our infrequent visits to the area where David lives, we found him camping with other homeless people in a redwood park. His face looked ten years older than his age, his hair was pulled up in a knot on the top of his head, and his dirty clothes were second-hand items from a local church. As we talked, I realized that my acute sense of pain was not just for the loss of my dreams for him but for the loss of the dreams he once had for himself.

Nevertheless, the next morning when we had breakfast together, I responded to his lifestyle in a way I would not have been able to do several years earlier. Before I would have seen his lifestyle as a judgment on me as a mother and would have reacted to my sense of guilt by trying once more to change him. This time I was simply curious about what he felt was his purpose in life. When he said his purpose was to teach macrobiotic diets to the homeless, I thought it a very strange occupation. But I didn't feel compelled to change his mind! In that moment I realized that *I had finally let go with love*, even though I did not understand or agree with his choices or lifestyle. I could see that he was someone with whom we may be involved only periodically, but who will always have a place in my heart.

Chapter 2

When Children March to Different Drummers

There have always been parents who have found it difficult to let go of adult children who have ignored the expectations their parents had for them. There have always been parents of "wayward" children who have tried to reshape their adult children into the form the parents originally wanted.

Today, however, the number of parents distressed over conflicts with their adult offspring seems to have increased. What is there about modern life that causes so many of us to question our parenting and the choices of our children? Why does it seem so difficult to let go?

There aren't any easy answers to those questions because no two situations are exactly alike. However, I can make some general observations.

For those of us who had our children back in "the good old days," the world of those far-off times seemed to move at a pace we could more easily handle. Mother could often afford to stay home and care for children full time. Parents were not as mobile; they often remained in the same community for several generations and so were able to draw upon the support of an extended family. Before the two-career household, parents had time to participate in children's extra-curricular activities, school events, and community affairs. And although it has never been a simple task for families to provide economic and emotional security for their children, success seemed almost assured for anyone with determination. In such a climate—before Vietnam and Woodstock—parents expected their offspring to follow their values without questioning, and many adult children did.

Those born after Vietnam clearly experienced a different culture from that of their parents. Their greater freedom, however, has not prevented them from having trouble letting go of *their* adult children—the "twentysomethings" who also march to a drum beat their parents did not play.

No matter when our children were born, we release them into a world different from the one in which we were raised. And the young adult being launched today faces a world in which there are more teen pregnancies and increased acceptance of single parenthood; neighbors who don't know one another; ethnic and racial isolation; unmarried couples openly living together, whether of the same sex or of the opposite sex; AIDS; guns in the classroom; random shots on the freeway; crack cocaine; gangs; downscaling of the economy; and on and on and on.

When we fail to let our children go freely into the world because they do not seem capable of being responsible adults, we may hope to put off the day they will have to be responsible on their own. We may assume—incorrectly, of course—that we can protect our children from the slings and arrows of outrageous fortune, especially during times that are difficult for the most responsible adult. In our attempt to protect, we prevent them from learning what they must learn if they are ever to be strong and independent individuals.

Some Parents Hide Their Disappointment

It is obvious that some parents *do* let go of their adult children even when the parents disagree with their children's values and choices. Despite their disappointment, they send their children into the world without needing to hover in the background. They can separate their values and the "success" of their own lives from the apparent "failure" and choices of their children.

But few of us who are disappointed in how our child has turned out (or who are afraid our child is heading in a direction likely to create problems later on) are *truly* able to let go. On the outside we may look like those parents who *have* let go. However, on the inside we hold on to our disappointment and to the hope that our child will make the choices we want him to make.

It is important to remember that *hiding our disappointment does not keep it from affecting us or our relationship with our children.*

A television drama, *Our Sons*, is an excellent illustration of the difficulties parents create for themselves and their children when they try to ignore the fact that their children have failed to fulfill their dreams, whether or not those dreams are realistic.

The story concerns Donald, a gay man who is dying of AIDS, and James, his lover. Donald's mother, Luanne, does not accept her son's gay lifestyle and has neither seen nor heard from him in fourteen years. Nevertheless, she finally decides to make peace with him.

James' mother, Audrey, on the other hand, prides herself on acceptance of her son's sexual preference. Soon, however, Luanne's simple, direct honesty forces Audrey to realize that she has not been honest with herself or with James.

Near the end of the drama, Audrey and James finally have a heart-to-heart talk in which she acknowledges that she was devastated when she first learned James was gay—admitting that it was a long time before she stopped hoping he'd see the true light, marry the girl of her dreams, and give her babies that would call her grandma and on whom she could lavish things. Angry that there was nothing she could do about her lost dreams, but feeling guilty for having them, she tried to pretend she was a woman of the world who could take it all in stride.

As Audrey tells her son the truth, she is embarrassed to discover that he had always known she was not the happy parent she claimed to be. After all, he says, "How could I not have heard the word you never spoke?" "What word?" she asks. "Disappointment," he responds. When she asks him why he didn't say anything, he points out that sometimes it's not wise to tell people what they don't want to know.

Audrey was like many parents who don't want to accept the fact that they are disappointed. They think they "shouldn't" feel disappointed. Perhaps they've listened to a colleague of mine who doesn't even like the phrase "disappointed parent." It is difficult for her to imagine that she will be disappointed in her children when they are launched into adulthood; until now her children have made choices with which she agrees. But as my sister-in-law, whose sons are clean-cut, high achievers, points out, "It's easy to let go when your children are doing what you'd like them to do."

That's exactly the point. There is a *big* difference between letting go when our children demonstrate an ability to navigate the intricacies of adulthood and when they can't or won't. It is also difficult not to get caught up in our expectations if they make choices that are far from the direction in which we thought we were steering them, no matter how successful their lives may appear to others.

Caught by Unmet Expectations

What was the direction in which you thought you were steering your child? What drum did you play?

Although you may not have thought of it at the time, you began playing your parental drum from the moment you and your spouse or partner decided to have a baby, the day you chose to adopt a child, the day you married someone who already had a child, or the moment you chose to keep a child even though you hadn't intended to get pregnant. The reason you did any of those things created the basic rhythm you played on your drum.

Did you want to expand your love of your mate by having a child who would be an expression of both of you? Or did you have a child to prevent a marriage from falling apart? Were all your friends having children and you didn't want to be left out? Did you have a child to prove to your mother that you could do a better job than she did? And was your family carefully planned, each child arriving when you could give it your greatest attention and love? Was the sex of the child terribly important?

Long before their baby is born, some parents discuss the values they want their child to have: integrity, a particular religious faith, education, a sense of responsibility. Other parents just assume that they will pass on their values when the time comes. They figure things will work out for them as well, if not better, than they did for their own parents.

We dispense our parental wisdom, hopes, and values, whether deliberately arrived at or not, while we spread jelly on our children's bread and pour milk into their cups. Unconsciously we impart our expectations as we interact with them in what may seem small and insignificant ways. Many years later we are reminded of those expectations, spoken and unspoken, when our children, through a combination of circumstance and choice, refuse to follow the blueprint we laid out for them.

You probably know highly educated parents who push their children to achieve academically. Since *they* have been successful by using their minds, they *assume* that formal education is an essential step in the development of responsible adults. But what if their son refuses to attend college? What if, instead, he wants to work his way around the world, doing odd jobs and taking pictures of his travels, which he hopes one day to sell? While the parents may be proud of their son's independence, they will most likely feel disappointed. Their educational values have been rejected and they may find it surprisingly hard to let go of their expectations.

You probably also know other parents who are not highly educated but who have been successful through hard work. Suppose such parents own a hardware store and have always *assumed* their son would carry on the family business. Suppose their son decides to become a cancer researcher. While they may be proud of their child's intelligence and ambition, they, too, will experience disappointment in abandoned plans for the business. They must now deal with an unexpected shift in their lives. When parents get hooked by what they *assume* will happen when their children grow up, they will be disappointed. And because they are disappointed, they will have a hard time letting go.

Gaps that Grow into Major Rifts

As long as there are generations there will be generation gaps, such as the one between parents who love classical music and offspring who enjoy (some claim to *understand*) hard rock. The potential for differences of opinion and values is almost limitless. Yet we usually learn to live with many of them.

For example, as I write this chapter all of our children are living with a significant other. In other words, they are doing what would have been called "shacking up" when I was young. As the daughter and granddaughter of ministers, I was taught that such behavior was scandalous. But times have changed, and I cannot force my children to follow the pattern of marry-first-and-live-together-later that I was raised to believe is best. Perhaps my way of doing things *is* better. Nevertheless, in this arena, this particular generation gap, I find I can accept the decisions of my children without many qualms.

However, as the first chapter illustrates, there are some generation gaps that can grow into significant rifts within our homes and hearts. Instead of minor differences that cause a few threads to unravel around the edges of the family's fabric, there is a tear straight down the middle. A few frayed edges are to be expected. A major rip is not.

To describe the atmosphere in my family for many years, and that experienced in the homes of some of my clients, I use the phrase "the rifts that bind." Since rifts would seem to pull people apart rather than bind them together, these words may seem incongruent. Let me explain.

"The ties that bind" refers to relationships in which people share history and/or similar values. In most families these ties are like an invisible rope of infinite length that connects parent and child. Whether living under the same roof or miles apart, parents and child hold the rope gently in their hands, knowing it reinforces their love and support for one another.

In families with strained relations, however, the rope represents broken dreams, blame, and failure. Standing on either side of the differences that divide them, parent and child hold tightly to their ends of the rope. They are bound not by *shared values* but by the realization that *their values are in conflict*, that the choices of the children are not supported by the parents and that the parents' expectations for the child are not going to be met. Each pulls on the rope in an attempt to manipulate the other. And the more tenaciously the other person defends his or her expectations of how things "should" be, the deeper the rift becomes. Technically speaking, the rift itself does not bind, but when we focus on the rift and on what separates us, we are bound and caught by our expectations that the other person should have different values than he or she has.

If you and your child have been playing tug-of-war across a growing rip in your family's fabric, my hope is that this book can help you learn how to stop tugging on that rope. In chapter 7 I describe how I dropped my end of the rope, and the peace that accompanied that action. I didn't give up my values and beliefs. I didn't give up the hope that David might someday decide to choose a more healthy lifestyle. I simply recognized that he and I may never resolve our differences and that pulling on the rope only caused my heart to break over the behavior of someone else—behavior I could not control.

You, too, can let go of the rope that binds you in misery and reminds you of your child's unfulfilled expectations. First, however, you may need to understand some of the dynamics that created the tug-of-war in the first place.

While almost any choice of an adult child that is inconsistent with our expectations can leave us disappointed and make it hard for us to let our child live freely as she chooses, three categories of situations most commonly lead to rifts that bind.

1. **Our child is unable to function successfully in relationships and/or work settings because of emotional and/or physical problems. The child's current functioning may be less than the potential demonstrated when our child was younger or may be a continuation of problems we have attempted to correct.**

If our child was handicapped from birth, or injured through illness or accident, the pain we feel is usually different from that experienced if our child previously demonstrated an ability to achieve and now fails to live up to that potential.

One of the parents I interviewed for this book expressed how it feels to be disappointed when great potential lies unfulfilled. Her brilliant son was addicted to cocaine. She said her therapist accurately expressed her pain when he said, "If you thought your son was so promising that he must surely have been sprinkled with fairy dust, and you have given him every opportunity to achieve success, his unwillingness to live up to that promise causes a deeper disappointment than if he hadn't seemed so special in the first place."

On the other hand, perhaps your daughter has had problems throughout her life. Despite your best efforts to help her with therapy, tutors, and extra attention, she doesn't seem able or willing to function to the degree you believe possible. It is not surprising that you would feel disappointed and very frustrated. You may say to yourself, "I've done my best; why can't she?"

A few examples of potential rifts in this category are drug and alcohol abuse, mental illness, suicide attempts, and handicaps caused by accidents or illness.

Incidentally, letting go in all of these cases is not easy. However, it is even more difficult when an adult child is not only unable to live responsibly herself but is also unable to be responsible for her children. Increasingly, parents who planned to retire are discovering they must re-enter the world of active parenting when grandchildren are dumped on their doorsteps.

2. Our child makes decisions concerning career, lifestyle, marriage, or parenting that are contrary to our values.

Because of television and the easy dissemination of information, our children have been exposed to a wider variety of options than most of us had when we were young. To add to this, the climate of our society encourages young people to make their own choices rather than have their parents choose for them. Consequently, there are almost unlimited ways in which our children might decide to follow a path that diverges from values we have comfortably held as "correct" for many years. Because we have not personally been exposed to some of these ideas and lifestyles, it can be very difficult for us to understand how our children could possibly make the choices they do.

Some examples of the ways our children's choices can cause us disappointment and distress are a change of religion; marriage outside our race, religion, or social group; divorce; having children without being married; abortion; political views extremely different from ours; not finishing college, or entering a career we believe unsuited to our child's talents; marriage to someone we feel will be harmful to the child in some way; being unable or unwilling to handle financial affairs responsibly; deciding to engage in illegal activities.

Many gays and lesbians, and sometimes their parents, do not consider homosexuality to be a conscious, deliberate choice, as are the other situations just listed. In fact, there are several studies indicating sexual preference has a strong biological component. Nevertheless, I include homosexuality in this category because gay and lesbian lifestyles are frequently experienced by parents as a rejection of parental and societal values. Learning that our child prefers members of his or her own sex requires a painful adjustment that most parents did not expect. It is not surprising that such parents keep pulling and tugging on the rope, trying to get their child to love those of the opposite sex so they can avoid dealing with the rift between their expectations and what their child feels.

3. Our child deliberately chooses to be emotionally and/or physically distant from us.

Almost all parents expect their children to stay in touch throughout life. If the child lives close to the parents, it is usually assumed that the child, and grandchildren, will visit often. On the other hand, if the child moves away from the home town, it is assumed the child will write, phone, or visit as often as possible. We may assume that our children will be there to take care of us in our old age—and in a manner we anticipate will give us pleasure.

When that doesn't happen, parents can feel very greatly pained.

I'm not talking here about the adult child who only calls once a week but whose parent thinks truly loving children would call every day. Nor am I referring to those children who are sometimes too busy to remember to send their mother a card on Mother's Day.

The child in this category has decided, for whatever reason, to break off contact with one or both parents. Perhaps he maintains some contact (his parents know where he lives, for instance, and he doesn't refuse their phone calls) but the visits are extremely rare and brief. The child may give no reason for his decision or may give a reason the parents don't understand. Sometimes the child will side with an ex-spouse, implying that full contact would be disloyal to the other parent.

The parent of these children is left standing on one side of a rift, holding her end of the rope that was *supposed* to connect her with her son. She feels unable to resolve her pain if her son is not willing or able to negotiate a different relationship.

Different Degrees of Pain

If the situation with your child fits one of the categories above, there are several factors that will determine whether you are only *somewhat* disappointed (making it potentially easier to stop tugging on the rope) or whether you find yourself in *great* distress, in which case letting go will be much more difficult. The first factor is your attitude concerning the seriousness of your child's "problem" and how intensely you believe your views are right and your child's are wrong; the second is the strength of the bond between you and your child; and the third is the coping skills and personality style you bring to conflicts and problems.

These variables can be expressed in a formula of A + B + C = D or:

$$\text{Attitudes} + \text{Bonds} + \text{Coping skills} =$$
$$\text{Degree of Disappointment and Pain}$$

Since you already know a little about me, let me tell you the story of Maria, a client of mine, before demonstrating how these factors interact in her situation and in mine.

Maria held a responsible middle-management job in a large company and considered herself a "liberated" woman who had successfully challenged the submissive role of many wives within the Mexican-American community in which she lived. Yet when her daughter Angela, an honors student, announced she was going to marry Kenji, a man who was raised in Japan and whose leg had been amputated after a car accident, Maria was amazed to discover her disappointment. Although she said nothing to Angela, her daughter read into her silence an attitude of prejudice and said that, if her mother couldn't accept Kenji just as her mother had accepted the husband of Angela's sister, she shouldn't attend the wedding.

While Maria felt pride in her daughter's willingness to marry someone with a physical handicap, her negative response to her future son-in-law's racial background was perplexing to her. "After all," she said, "I come from an ethnic minority. I headed a committee to bring more minorities into the PTA. Why do I suddenly feel like a racist?" It didn't take much probing to uncover the first, and primary, layer of her distress.

If Angela married Kenji, her grandchildren would look "different." They might not be accepted by all of her relatives, a large and exuberant group who used almost any occasion as an excuse to get together. Could Maria, or Angela, handle that rejection? Yet that was only one situation out of many potential problems Maria doubted her daughter had considered.

As Maria used the therapy setting to look more closely at her reactions, she decided to write down every objection and fear she could uncover. Soon she had more than a dozen. Her

*concerns ranged from the personal (would Kenji like Maria's
ethnic cooking?) to the obvious (would differences between her
son-in-law's culture and her daughter's cause problems for
them after the honeymoon glow faded?). One concern seemed
more serious to Maria: she was afraid her son-in-law might
not want to come to her house for the holidays, as all her other
children did. When she realized that she "strongly resented
having to adjust to that potential reality," we discovered the
underlying source of her pain—adjustment.*

*At work Maria was involved in another management
change, the third in a year. Her home had seemed a safe haven,
a place where change was not imposed upon her by someone
else. Now she wondered whether she had the energy to handle
another situation that was out of her hands. She knew that,
deep down, she would love her grandchildren no matter what
they looked like and that her daughter had the strength to make
a mixed-race marriage work. Maria decided that what she
needed was to find a way to handle the stress from her job so
that it didn't spill over into her family life.*

*After role-playing with me on how she could approach
Angela and Kenji, she took them to dinner. She was very relieved by what they had to say. For one thing, they assured her
they had already discussed potential problems and had decided
they would handle difficulties as they arose. Kenji teased Maria, saying she could call him "Ken" if that made him seem
less Oriental. Maria decided "Kenji" was just fine with her
and the marriage went off without a hitch.*

Our Attitudes and Beliefs

An attempted suicide by an adult child (or an attempt that is, unfortunately, successful) is experienced by all parents as extremely
painful. Yet situations that are far less life-threatening can be viewed
by some parents as equally tragic.

There are two reasons why some parents can view the rift with
their child as undesirable, but not overwhelming, and others consider
a similar rift to be unbearable. The first reason has to do with how
damaging we consider our child's "problem" is now, or will be in the
future, either physically, financially, emotionally, or socially. The second reason has to do with our willingness to accept our child's functioning at a lower level than we know our child is capable of achieving.

For example, a child who is manic-depressive can create a great
deal of trauma and distress in a family. However, her parents, while

clearly disappointed that they have to adjust to changes in moods, are unlikely to consider the problem a rift that cannot be tolerated if they view her illness as *biological* and gently encourage her use of medication. On the other hand, if her parents view her mood swings as *psychological*, they may blame her for being emotionally unstable; then their attempts to force her into treatment may be driven by anger that she doesn't take responsibility for her actions. However, if they castigate themselves for causing her mental instability, their efforts to help her will be driven by guilt. Unfortunately, both anger and guilt will deepen the rift between them.

If our child chooses to open a wood-working shop or a gas station, we may be tickled pink because of his initiative or extremely depressed because we think manual labor is beneath the standards of our family. As long as we believe he should have found a "better" occupation, we will be reluctant to accept his choice of professions.

The extent to which the choices of children can pull generations apart depends, in large measure, upon the rigidity with which both parent and child hold certain opinions to be "right." We pull on the rope across the rift not so much because our child has different opinions and behaviors than we do but because we place positive or negative values on those opinions and behaviors. When an adult child wants to return home because she can't pay her rent, some parents are pleased to help out, wishing they could do even more; others will be distressed because they believe adult children must be independent and self-sufficient.

✦　✧　✦

How does this variable apply to Maria's situation and to mine?

Maria did not believe that mixed marriages are necessarily "wrong," only that they present challenges she was unsure her daughter could handle. Angela's welfare and Maria's desire not to have to adjust to another change are the real issues, not a rigid belief in the separation of races. If the latter had been her position, her pain would have been much more acute. Resolution would then have been difficult, or impossible, as long as Angela chose to pursue her plans for marriage.

In my situation, David's chemical dependency was extremely painful because I know that alcohol and drug abuse not only creates problems in relationships and work—it can also kill. Although today he seems to have cut back on the chemicals he puts into his body, at times he has acknowledged that he may "possibly" be addicted. Nevertheless, he does not believe he needs help. Certainly he doesn't think he's "hit bottom." I don't understand why that is so. It would seem to me that when he lived on the streets it would have been obvious that his life was not working very well. That would be considered "bottom" by many!

In addition to my reaction to David's chemical addiction, I am very upset by the fact that he does not have a job. If I believed that he had a physical or mental condition that clearly prevented him from functioning in a work situation, my pain perhaps would not be quite as great. However, I suspect he shares the attitude of many in his generation who have dropped out, or who see no need to expend much energy in working. Support from the government means he doesn't have to. Whatever the case may be, I am upset because I strongly believe that people need to be financially responsible for their own lives, if at all possible.

Our Bond of Love and Shared History

The blueprint for survival of the human species includes a unique connection between parents and the child who is entrusted to their care by birth or adoption. That solid bond is probably essential if we are to get through the rough spots without periodically wanting to sell our child to the highest bidder.

This bond of love is formed in many ways. Often it begins in the delivery room when our baby is held up for us to see and our eyes fill with tears of joy we didn't know possible. Our heart beats faster when we are drawn to the picture of one particular child among several offered for adoption, the child we will welcome into our home as one of our own. We see the smudged face of our boyfriend's little boy and it is love at first sight. Yet even when parents do not bond so quickly or so intensely, they almost always love their child.

The ease with which we bond (and the intense experience of that bond) does not guarantee, of course, that we will be excellent parents; nor does it prevent us from being abusive parents. There is much evidence that decent parenting can occur when parents don't feel particularly well connected with their offspring. There are also many cases in which parents who have a suffocating attachment to their young child can seriously damage that child's need for autonomy and healthy independence when he becomes an adult.

Because of the unique relationship we have with our child, as she grows we have an intrinsic interest in everything she does: her friends, her success at school, her talents, her shortcomings. Our interest and our desire to have her be a significant part of our lives can continue even after she has reached the age of maturity and even though she may want to do something of which we disapprove.

✦ ✧ ✦

Maria has always felt very close to her children. The dynamic in their home is described by family therapists by the term "centripetal." Such families tend to pull children into the home and its atmosphere. The parents feel very uncomfortable and experience great loss when their children move out of the area, except for temporary activities such as college or a tour of duty in the armed services. Other families encourage, even force, their children to leave the nest. Such families are called "centrifugal." In these homes the dynamics tend to mitigate against disappointment when children choose mates unlike the family; disengagement is expected.

Since Maria placed a premium on closeness and harmony, she experienced more discomfort. The fact that her daughter was getting married was okay—as long as she returned for every holiday and participated with her siblings in family gatherings. But fears that her son-in-law might not be willing to insist that Angela remain connected with the family caused Maria great distress. She wasn't sure she could handle a rupture in the bond with her daughter, a bond she considered essential to her identity as a mother.

The bond I expected always to feel with my children also caused me great unhappiness as the rift grew in our family. My pediatrician was a kind old gentleman who, on the first visit to his office after my babies were born, had a special technique that reinforced the bond I already felt with my new child. He would hold the baby firmly under the arms and would lift him or her off the table to observe the baby's muscle tone. At that point in the exam he would always say, "We will dream great dreams for you."

Although my doctor probably said that to all his patients, I felt that somehow he had seen into the recesses of my heart and, in expressing the dreams I felt, assured their success. I also felt that I had been given a mandate to make certain those dreams came true. For perhaps the first five or six years of our difficulties with David, I could not tell that story without a lump in my throat and tears in my eyes. In remembering my intention to dream great dreams for our son, I felt overwhelmed because I believed I had failed to make those dreams a reality.

Our Coping Skills and Personality Style

Personalities, temperaments, and coping skills obviously differ greatly from individual to individual. We do well, therefore, to remember that our reaction to differences between us and our child is not necessarily the reaction *all* parents would have in that situation. Knowing others are less distressed may give us courage to learn new ways of reacting to our child and to build new strengths in our personalities, strengths that will lessen our pain.

Imagine a situation in which a young woman living with her parents decides to join a church different from the one her parents belong to, although it is within the same religion, because she likes the other pastor better. Parents who accept change easily will probably be unhappy that their daughter won't share church activities with them, but will otherwise not feel upset. Parents who do not adjust well to change and who tend to take everything personally, however, might consider their daughter's decision to change churches as an affront to *them*, whether or not they say anything. Each parent's distress is affected by the way in which she is able to adjust to new situations and by her ability to encourage and tolerate independence.

Maria had great personal strength, illustrated in part by her ability to maintain an active family life and also hold a responsible position requiring long hours at work. Her self-identity came from *many* sources, not just the image she had of herself as mother. She usually did not take on responsibility that belonged to her children, although in this case she did worry about whether Angela could handle future problems.

All in all, Maria's personality structure mitigated against extreme pain. She felt moderate discomfort over a situation she didn't know how to handle. She might have been deeply distressed if she had focused all her energy on her family. Then she might have wondered what she had done "wrong" to cause her daughter to select Kenji.

Even before the seriousness of David's situation was clear, I had begun to stop swimming upstream in my perfectionistic attempt to be in control of situations that were not within my power to control. As I became more successful in that effort, my distress over my inability to change David gradually became less and less.

Because I have always been motivated to be a "better" person, I was focused on trying to "fix" the rift in our family, even though my attempts often floundered. Over time, however, I noticed that things were a little different, a little less tense. It wasn't David who changed, which is what I first wanted, of course. Instead, change gradually occurred as I learned to accept the reality that I wasn't able to make David change. Nevertheless, the fact that movement was happening at all gave me hope that there could be light at the end of the tunnel.

Different Expressions of Disappointment

Just as our personalities determine the *amount of distress* we will experience, our personalities affect *how we respond*. In almost all cases our response will be a variation on one of four themes.

Anger and Blame Openly Directed Against Our Child

In my experience, disappointed fathers react to rifts in the family with anger and blame more frequently than do mothers. They may let their child know directly, and often loudly, of this displeasure. Or they may simply distance themselves from their child with the silence of unspoken accusations.

There are several reasons men respond with anger and blame more than women. The first is probably that males are, generally, more comfortable with anger than they are with expressions of sadness and regret. They often attempt to cover their pain with anger by blaming the child for the family's turmoil. Women, on the other hand, have been socialized to deny their anger and to focus on relationships, smoothing things over.

Another reason mothers do not respond to family rifts with as much anger as fathers (although there are always exceptions) is, I believe, because mothers *generally* tend to bond more closely with their children than do fathers. This is not to suggest that men don't feel a deep connection with their children. But mothers get a nine-month head start on the bonding process. They've been carrying their child long before their husband has the pleasure of holding and rocking a baby. Mothers, therefore, are less likely to pour oil on the fire by showing their anger (even when they feel it), because they are afraid expressions of anger will further erode an essential bond that already seems frayed.

The most important reason that women don't respond with anger and blame, however, is because they feel much more guilty than men do. Their guilt drives them to use the next common response to disappointment and family rifts, constant pressure on the child in an attempt to get him to change his ways.

Nagging Fueled by Guilt

If you respond to disappointment in your child by frequently offering comments and suggestions for how he should live his life, you are not alone. You may call what you do "showing an interest in my child" and "just stating my opinion." Your child recognizes it for what it is, "nagging."

When we are stuck in a *parent-to-child* relationship, our "suggestions" easily take on the tone of nagging and manipulation. This is not surprising. We think we understand our child's vulnerabilities—and what he should do to overcome them. We know there are always pitfalls and dangers lying ahead to snare the unwary. After all, we've been around the block a few times and have made more than a few mistakes of our own. We want to prevent our child from going through what we experienced.

Consequently, if coercion and frequent reminders were our favorite techniques in getting our child to change when he was young, we will probably continue to use that approach in our attempts to reverse the direction in which our adult child is moving. With efforts both subtle and direct, we encourage our child to be more responsible, to enter a treatment program or to stop living with that no-good character. We lose sleep, money, and time in our efforts to form our child into the shape we want. Seldom do we see much progress for our efforts, but we continue trying "for the sake of our child."

If the truth be known, we often continue as much for *our* sake as for the benefit of our child. The reason is not because we are narcissistic and don't want our child to have a life of his own. But we parents have been sold a bill of goods. We have been told that parents, especially mothers, have the power to affect our child's personality and lifestyle to a great degree. When we buy this myth and our grown child doesn't "turn out" as we think he should, we assume it is our fault. We are afraid we won't get our good parent badge until he turns out "right." So we keep nagging in the hope that things will change and we won't feel like failures.

Passive Hope and Crying in Our Beer

Some disappointed parents don't get angry. They don't nag. They simply throw up their hands in resignation and claim there is "nothing" they can do. There is, of course. They could work on exploring *why* they can't let go freely. Unfortunately, they think they have given their child freedom to choose her own life. *But their gift of "letting go" is attached to the not-well-hidden proviso that she should choose what they know is best for her.* This passive tactic seldom works any better than direct nagging and expressions of anger.

Nevertheless, these parents are left with a vague hope that things will, somehow, work out. They maintain a vigil for signs of "improvement," signs that their child will make the changes they want her to make. When that doesn't happen, they settle deeper and deeper into their side of the rift that separates them from their daughter. They may not jerk the rope, but they also won't let go.

The passivity of some parents is worn like a hair shirt they display at every opportunity. They become experts in playing the martyr, releasing deep sighs meant to influence their audience; sighs that seem to say, "After all we've done for her, you'd think she'd be able to see what's best for her." Their sighs have no effect, of course, on getting their daughter to see things differently. But what is even more unfortunate, their sighs prevent their hearts from healing.

Unable or unwilling to address differences in values with their child openly and directly, a process that might resolve those differences, they have no good outlet for their distress. Such parents often develop physical and emotional problems that are difficult to solve. After all, it is hard to cure an ailment in which symptoms are far removed from the cause.

Acceptance

This last response of parents to disappointment in their adult children is characteristic of those who focus their attention on developing what can be called an *adult-to-adult relationship* with their child. They don't waste time in anger, blame, guilt, or vacant hope. When they express honest differences of opinion, they aren't nagging. They respect the right of their child to have different views. They may even have heated discussions but they don't indulge in pointless arguments. And while they may offer suggestions on what their child might do to resolve a problem, they make it clear that it is the child's right and responsibility to make a final decision.

This book is all about how you can become this kind of parent. You, too, can learn to accept your child and to let go with love, even though your child's functioning in life and her choices have helped create painful rifts in the family.

✦ ✧ ✦

In looking at the four ways parents express their disappointment in how things have turned out, we can look again at Maria's and my situation.

Maria's personality clearly shaped the way she responded to Angela's engagement. Her independent nature and desire to solve problems by herself led her, initially, to keep her opinions hidden. She seldom expressed anger and was afraid that telling Angela she was upset might cause her daughter to pull away from her. Since she had not been an overbearing mother when the children were young, nagging to keep Angela from marrying Kenji was not her style. It was her strength of character that gave her the courage to discuss her concerns with me, even though acknowledgment of her views opened her to the possibility that I might consider her prejudiced.

As I discussed in the first chapter, both Bob's personality and mine played major roles in shaping the way we responded to David's drug and alcohol use—laying the foundation for an eventual rift between him and us. When it had become a full-blown problem, Bob was able to cut himself off emotionally better than I could. Since he doesn't often get angry, he didn't waste a lot of time ranting and complaining. He also didn't blame others, simply believing that David was responsible for his actions once he became an adult.

For the first several years after David began using drugs, my primary technique was guilt-driven manipulation. I would try more and more subtle devices to get him to change. None worked. Finally, I decided to give up trying. However, stopping was not as easy as I expected. Just as ocean liners can continue moving forward for a great distance after the engines are reversed, the inertia of my old habits sometimes caused me to continue trying to change David long after I decided to stop.

Keeping Our Troubles to Ourselves

When a group of parents who have adult children get together, there will almost always be those whose children have not "turned out" as expected. Yet often others in the group may not suspect that anything is wrong. Why? A few parents, of course, will not say anything because they are like Audrey, mentioned at the start of this chapter, and think they "should" be accepting of their children. Others, however, clearly know they are unhappy; they are just reluctant to discuss their family's situation openly. Perhaps they come from homes where they were warned about "hanging the family's dirty laundry in public." They believe they have to keep their troubles to themselves.

If their pain becomes intense, however, they may reach out to a friend, pastor or therapist. Even then, they may avoid discussing their problem by talking about the stress they feel at work, the trouble they are having with a car repair project, worry over a spouse's health or a running feud with noisy neighbors. They are like the mother killdeer, a bird who distracts intruders by pretending her wing is broken, hoping to prevent them from noticing her babies in a nearby nest. They can be quite inventive in designing ways to distract others, and themselves, from seeing the pain in their heart because it is too great. And so the pain remains hidden, unable to be touched and healed by understanding and support from others.

In addition to the taboo some parents have against sharing family difficulties, there are many other reasons disappointed parents hide their feelings from those outside the family (and often within the circle of their own relatives). Here are some of the reasons parents have given me for failing to tell others of their pain.

- They may be embarrassed by the actions of their child—and embarrassment tends to keep anyone quiet.

- After struggling for years to resolve a problem within the family, they may not have the energy to rehash old wounds. Besides, they figure it won't do any good. What could someone else possibly suggest? They have tried everything.

- They expect others will judge them as harshly, or more harshly, than they already judge themselves.

- Their pain may simply be too close to the surface to trust others with it. Typical is the mother whose son had problems similar to those we had with ours. She came up to me after a talk I had given, impressed that I could openly discuss our family's situation, and said, "I think sometimes that telling others about my son could help me, but I always cry when I use his name." Her eyes glistened with tears as she spoke.

- There are times when parents are distracted from the rift with their child by other pressing issues that take center stage, such as tending to the serious illness of a family member.

Even though I freely told my worries about David to friends, for a long time I was very careful around others. I avoided parents who had raised highly successful children with what appeared to be little effort. Others to be avoided were those who would tell me about friends whose children were worse off than David and those who, in an attempt to make me feel better, would insist that "everything will work out fine." It doesn't help a toothache sufferer to know that at any given moment there are millions of other toothache sufferers in the world. It didn't help to be told that *eventually* David would see the light. So far that hasn't happened; at least he hasn't seen the light I would like him to notice. Discouraging parents from feeling their pain does not make it go away.

On the other hand, there are those who have helped diminish my pain by listening with an open heart. I particularly remember a woman I met five years ago at a workshop we attended. Several of us went to lunch together and were talking about our families. As I shared about David, she said, "You must hurt a lot. I don't know what I would do if I were in your shoes." Her understanding words were like a gentle hug, deeply touching my heart. They didn't change my situation one bit. My son still had his problems. I still didn't know what else to do. However, for the moment at least, I realized that I didn't need to carry my pain alone.

If you are having trouble letting others know how you feel, I encourage you to open your heart so others can share your burden. You may even discover solutions you had not considered.

Chapter 3

The Parenting Game

Everyone who chooses to raise a child is automatically enrolled in The Parenting Game. The goal is to maneuver, with love and minimum error, a small but growing object through a series of increasingly complex mazes that end after eighteen years have passed. The skills required? Simple. You only need patience, strength, wisdom, sacrifice, courage, perseverance, flexibility, nurturance, love, loyalty, and a good dose of humor.

Different rules have been carefully prepared for mothers and fathers by other parents, family members, friends, and, of course, by legions of "experts." If the mother does not play according to the prevailing standards of the rule makers, she is penalized. Fathers, on the other hand, are provided with handicaps that allow them to participate at their own discretion and drop out without severe penalty. However, as the game progresses both parents must constantly be prepared for revised rules that may contradict earlier ones. No one can ever be fully prepared for The Parenting Game.

How does it feel to play that challenging contest? Suzanne Gordon expresses a typical response when she talks of being a parent, "the identity that can never be shed." In a recent commentary in the *Los Angeles Times* she wrote:

> *I know from personal experience that the intense work of parenting does not end after a few exhausting months of round-the-clock feeding and diapering . . . I know it involves far more than teaching children to "go potty," feed themselves, read, write, and think, respect other human beings, control hostility and anger, overcome sadness and disappointment, forge close relationships with others, and maybe someday find a mate and have children of their own . . . It involves the extraordinary capacity to cope with one's own frustration—and sometimes even one's own rage—to balance one's own needs with the often un-*

*predictable needs of another, to tolerate terrible anxiety and
even dread about their safety and well-being, to give and give
and give when there is no "please" and "thank you," and finally, in such a bittersweet finale, to let go.*

The Finger of Guilt Points to Mother

At the moment the last maze is completed and The Parenting Game
is over, how parents will evaluate their performance will depend primarily upon two things. One, is the parent a mother or a father? Two,
is the parent satisfied with the grown child who has reached the end
of the playing field?

If the answer to the first question is "mother" and the latter
"no," her turmoil will generally be greater than if her husband re-
views the game, even if the answer for him is also "no." John
Rosemond, a psychologist who writes for the *Charlotte Observer*, notes
that regardless of marital status, many women, if not most, are encouraged to believe that success of the child-rearing process rests "on their
shoulders and their shoulders alone."

Part of the idea that mothers are responsible for their offspring
arises from our depiction of mothers as "angels," as we can readily
read in almost any Mother's Day card. This perspective proclaims
mothers to be fonts of endless nurturance, sacrifice, wisdom, and love,
possessing a strong but gentle ability to raise children because they
are blessed with estrogen and willingly suppress their own needs.
From the pulpit and parenting magazines come glowing accolades for
the hands that rock the cradle.

There isn't room, apparently, for us mothers to be ordinary people—for opposed to the "angel" view is the "witch" perspective, as
negative as the first is flattering. According to this concept, mothers
neglect and mistreat their children because they want to live through
them and are either overbearing and overprotective or lacking in ma-
ternal attention. A hundred ills of society are laid at the feet of these
lesser mortals.

Paula J. Caplan, Ph.D., is a spokesperson for a more balanced
perspective. Her book *Don't Blame Mother* illustrates how experts create and perpetuate the belief that mother is responsible for how The
Parenting Game turns out. She reports that she and a graduate student read 125 articles in nine major mental health journals from 1970
to 1982. Regardless of the author's sex or occupation as psychiatrist,
psychologist, or other mental health professional, mothers were
blamed for 72 different kinds of problems in their offspring. These
ranged from bed-wetting to schizophrenia, from inability to deal with

color blindness to learning problems and homicidal transsexualism, whatever that is.

Caplan also described the strait jacket we place around some particularly unfortunate, hard-working mothers. These are the wives of alcoholics, drug addicts, compulsive gamblers, and womanizers. The mothers supposedly make life hard for their children by supporting their husband's addictions and compulsions and are given the pathologizing label "co-dependent." They are accused of doing too much and, at the same time, of failing to save their children from their father's addictive behavior. Yet the irony is that, if they leave their husbands, they are blamed for breaking up the family and depriving the children of their father.

Few disappointed mothers fail to absorb at least *some* of a deluge of theory and opinion about their power to influence their child's life. Because there is a bit of truth in even the most outlandish ideas, we take to heart the "rules" for mother. Our *mea culpa* demonstrates how easily we assume it is always us, the mothers, who cause our child's problems or who have failed to teach higher values. Even mothers whose children completed The Parenting Game to their satisfaction often question whether they did the job "right."

For example, Mildred, a mother I interviewed, has three grown sons who are psychologically healthy and hold responsible jobs. However, she still reflects upon the day thirty years ago when her son, then four, was particularly annoying, being a pest as only four-year-olds know how to be. At her wits' end, she locked him in the garage, saying, "Until you can be part of the family, you will stay in here." Although he came out later and was reunited with a loving family, Mildred's questioning of her action reflects the common belief that there is a "best way" to respond to every situation. Surely another mother—with greater wisdom or patience—would have thought of something else, something "better."

Fewer Expectations for Father

Where was our husband when we were delegated the more demanding rules for parenting? Did he request equal responsibility? Not likely, if he were a typical father.

While we changed diapers, monitored children's squabbles, cleaned house and chauffeured children to their activities, he was doing work for which he was *paid*, making it *more important* work. And the U.S. Department of Labor encouraged him to believe that the mother's job was not only less important than his, but less difficult too. That's because the primarily male civil servants in this bureaucracy (at least at the time most of us were raising our children the management was male) rated occupations according to the degree of complexity needed to handle "data," "people," and "things." It is not surprising that a brain surgeon required almost the highest level of skill. What is amazing, however, is that the job of a homemaker was considered to need only as much skill as that of a parking lot attendant and a horse pusher (that's a person whose job it is to feed, water, and otherwise tend horses traveling by train). Incidentally, a dog pound attendant and even a poultry offal worker supposedly required *greater* skills than homemakers, nursery school teachers, and foster parents. With pressure from the women's liberation movement and a study by the University of Wisconsin in 1975, the department's *Dictionary of Occupational Titles* was forced to upgrade homemakers somewhat. However, many families operated for years under the assumption that the work of the parent inside the home was not nearly as difficult or important as the work of the parent outside the home.

However, when we *did* work outside the home out of economic necessity or because we wanted to make use of our education, it was presumed that we, rather than our husband, would take time off work when our children were sick. And mothers were expected to handle the bulk of household responsibilities (including child care, of course) when they returned at the end of the day from office or factory.

Until recently, there has been a taboo against father blaming, except in cases of extreme abuse. Since father spent less time and emotional energy on the family, the children didn't *expect* him to be more involved—and didn't criticize him for his lack of involvement. The mother, however, was more available, or *expected* to be more available. Consequently, she became the target of children's frustrations, of their unmet needs and wants. If she gave her children 80 percent of her energy, they could still feel deprived because it *should* have been 100 percent.

Society's willingness to let fathers off the hook does not mean, of course, that a father is not distressed when a child doesn't meet his expectations. However, since fathers are not held as *accountable* for their child's situation, they do not generally feel as *responsible*.

A more balanced role for mothers and fathers in the future will require adjustment, as illustrated in a *Doonesbury* comic strip by Gary Trudeau. The story line concerns Rick, the father of four-year-old Jeff. Rick is about to fall asleep when his wife asks, "Rick, I know you love Jeff as much as I do. So why don't you seem as torn up about not being able to spend time with him?" Rick responds, "Well, it may be because I'm spending a whole lot more time on family than my father did, and you're spending far less time than your mother did. Consequently, you feel incredibly guilty, while I naturally feel pretty proud of myself. I think that's all it really amounts to, don't you?" He ends with, "Try to get some sleep, Baby . . ." as she reaches for a lamp to throw at him.

Guilt and the Advice of Experts

A significant cause of guilt concerning how well we play The Parenting Game can be traced to our reliance on the wisdom of experts. Unlike animals who can rely on instinct for raising their young, humans often need advice to get them through the Parenting Game, or simply to understand what the rules are. And at two o'clock in the morning when the new mother can't get her colicky baby to stop crying, she is thankful that she can reach for a baby care manual.

Society as a whole can also be thankful for professionals who devote their lives to helping both parents and children. With the encouragement of family therapists and child care advocates, we are beginning to tackle seriously the profound consequences of physical, sexual, and emotional abuse, problems swept under the rug for too many years.

There is no doubt that most of us are better parents because of what we have learned from experts. However, discovering *which* particular advice we should take is a tricky matter because different experts offer different views. Opinions vary according to the theoretical perspective of the author and where the pendulum is swinging on any given topic at the time we need advice. Consequently, it is not easy to know whether we've played The Parenting Game right or wrong, as illustrated in changing theories on the cause of schizophrenia.

For many years it was assumed that poor parenting created this devastating mental illness. One of the theories that supported this view was expounded by Murray Bowen, a prominent family systems theoretician. In describing the dynamics of family interactions, he suggested that a cause of schizophrenia could be explained in his observation that children have different levels of ability to disengage from what he called their "family ego mass" (which can be described as the way in which family members relate to one another).

Bowen said that those who were unable to separate from their families successfully tended to marry others who are likewise "undifferentiated" and immature. When the pattern of less-mature-marrying-less-mature continued for even as few as three generations, Bowen claimed that the immaturity of the parents could (although not necessarily would) produce a schizophrenic child. His view was added to those of others who also believed schizophrenia was caused by ineffective parenting.

Today, however, researchers have discovered strong evidence of a biological component to the disease, necessitating a rethinking of its cause. As one researcher suggests, the origins may lie in a trauma to the developing brain in the womb. These new theories do not mean that parents play no role in all cases of schizophrenia. But for many years parents believed that they *alone* were responsible for their child's debilitating illness, and they struggled with overwhelming guilt.

It is now clear that in the attempt to develop a theory about families, Murray Bowen unintentionally did a disservice to parents of schizophrenics. Nevertheless, some of his ideas have helped other parents.

For example, he developed a concept called "the multi-generational transmission process." This term is not familiar to many parents but it accurately describes the way in which we learn to play The Parenting Game. As we were growing up, we observed the family rituals, values, and attitudes that were modeled by our parents. Likewise, *our* parents decided what seemed right to them by watching *their* parents and absorbing values from the culture and social mores of that generation. And on and on into the past.

Since all families have their share of craziness and common sense, of rigidity and flexibility, of unresolved issues and effective methods of resolving conflict, part of what we learned from our family made it difficult to steer our children through some mazes in The Parenting Game, and part of what we learned made the game easier to play. Recognizing this fact should give us hope. If our behaviors have been learned, they can be changed. We don't have to keep passing down from generation to generation those behaviors and attitudes that have been unintentionally harmful to those we love.

Psychobabble and Guilt

Every profession has its jargon of words and phrases. Psychologists and other mental health professionals are no different. When used appropriately, these shortcuts to complex ideas provide a language that helps us better understand human behavior and thought. When applied inappropriately, however, they confuse and complicate the very issue they are intended to address—and create a condition called "psychobabble."

A good example of this occurred during an interview I had with a father of several grown children. In talking about one of his daughters, he said that he was "co-dependent" in allowing her to use his apartment for three months while she looked for a place of her own.

Furthermore, he said he felt badly about "enabling" her, but didn't know what else to do.

I was surprised that he would use those terms to describe his situation. From my perspective "co-dependency" describes a people pleaser who denies her own needs in order to focus on meeting the needs of others. "Enablers" are those who allow others to continue their self-destructive, addictive behaviors by making excuses for them and by other actions that prevent the addicts from being responsible for themselves. As far as I could see, he was neither co-dependent nor an enabler. He was simply assisting an adult child in need. It would be a far different matter if he couldn't afford to have her stay with him or she took unfair advantage of his hospitality. If we are afraid of offering needed help to our children because we think we might be labeled an "enabler," we fail to listen to the wisdom of our heart.

Other psychobabble terms that have been increasingly misused recently are "toxic parents," "dysfunctional," and "abuse."

Everywhere you look it seems as though almost any psychological conflict or problem is said to have its roots in inadequate parenting, as though the actions and inactions of parents were the *only* factor that influenced the behavior, emotions, and values of our adult children. Some people, such as John Bradshaw, have claimed that *96 percent* of American families are "dysfunctional" and that their children are "the children of trauma." Parents are often considered "toxic" to the health of their children.

Has almost every parent really done that poorly in The Parenting Game? Certainly none of us has had the skill to guide our child accurately through every maze. We are all in some way "impaired" and unable to always "function completely," two of the definitions that define dysfunction. However, the dictionary also defines dysfunction as "abnormal." Wait a minute. Surely 96 percent of families cannot be *ab*-normal, since "normal" implies something is usual or average. Are we all below average? If so, the meaning of the word is turned upside down. Or are we being judged by such high standards that nearly every parent deserves an "F" on the parent score card?

Yes, there are parents who have directly damaged their children through sexual, physical, and emotional abuse. Alcoholic parents *can* create lifelong problems for their children. Other parents *can* prevent their offspring from functioning as healthy adults if they suffocate them with extreme overprotection. And it would be nice if every parent could *always* recognize his child's needs and respond with appropriate nurturance and provide gentle but firm discipline.

The truth is that the vast majority of parents are ordinary people who bring many different skills, personalities, experiences—and inadequacies—to the role of parenting. Most of us do a poor job in some areas and a decent, even outstanding, job in others. Donald Winicott, a prominent clinician, uses the phrase "good-enough parenting" to describe what most of us do. Although this perspective is preferable to the "good" versus "bad" view of parenting, it seems to me that "good enough" still involves a value judgment that can be somewhat troublesome. I prefer the phrase "uneven parenting" as a description for what happens in *most* homes. We should reserve the term "dysfunctional," if a label must be used, for families of serious abuse.

Fortunately, critics outside the field of therapy and therapists themselves are beginning to question the overuse of "abuse" and "dysfunctional," or at least the counterproductive effect these labels can have on families. It is interesting to note that a recent lecture by Bradshaw was titled, "Blaming Mom and Dad: Has it gone too far?" Maybe he's getting the message. If so, this is welcome news. Bradshaw has certainly been a leading contributor to the psychobabble lexicon—albeit with the best of intentions.

When *are* psychological terms appropriate in describing parenting? And when is parenting not "uneven" but truly harmful to a growing child?

Many therapists help their clients heal the pain of genuine abuse by using these terms. They believe that clients who get in touch with memories of parental incest *need to see their experience as abusive*—which it was!—and *abnormal*—which it was! By holding on to the word "abusive," these clients often feel stronger if they choose to confront their parents with their pain and anger. Other clients may realize that a parent's frequent statement that "I wish you were never born" played a significant role in their depression and thoughts of suicide. These individuals see their parents as *emotionally* abusive—which they were! And there are parents whose interactions with their children can certainly be experienced as "toxic" if the children have developed no defenses to counter constant criticism and heavy-handed manipulation.

It is understandable for therapists to fear that labeling such therapeutic terms as "psychobabble" can become a way for parents to avoid admitting really serious mistakes in parenting.

Well, it would be nice if all parents who have *really* been abusive to their children would stand up and apologize, even though they may not have intended to hurt their child. After all, although apologies can't change the past, they can allow the person who was abused to feel that her pain is understood and that understanding can help her heal more quickly. In my experience, however, parents who have been abusive in the classic sense seldom acknowledge the full impact of their past behavior, if at all. It takes a *long* time and a *great* deal of courage for such parents to admit their mistakes. Those of us who already feel guilty for our *uneven parenting* can, unfortunately, become defensive in the face of our children's accusations if they are accompanied by extreme and negative labels.

The issue for us as parents who are disappointed in a grown child—and who wish to stop the family tug-of-war—is to acknowledge that, while we don't like the labels our child may use, we still need to be honest with ourselves. We must somehow find the courage to look at the various ways we affected our child's current problems or at how we influenced her interpretation of childhood events. For those parents willing to be honest, the second part of this book offers many suggestions for ways they can explore their role as parents— without guilt or labels.

What Satisfied Parents Have to Say

Despite the potential for guilt and a parenting game fraught with pitfalls, why are so many parents satisfied with how things turn out? Are their standards lower than those of parents disappointed in the results? Is there something they know that we don't?

Operating on the proposition that "satisfied parents" might have something to teach "disappointed parents," I interviewed dozens of parents whose relationships with grown children were clearly adult-to-adult. In these families there was mutual admiration and respect expressed by both parents and children. Most of the children held responsible jobs or were likely to move up the ladder of success eventually. A few of them had chosen not to pursue the careers they were capable of achieving, yet their lack of ambition did not particularly bother the parents. Several sons were openly gay.

Often claiming that they didn't know what they did "right," the parents were humble concerning their contributions to the sense of responsibility and psychological health of their children. However, their stories lead to some interesting observations, not the least of which is that there is no correct way to raise children. These "successful" parents shared no single, outstanding trait or parental decision that could be interpreted as *the magic ingredient* every parent needs when playing, or analyzing, The Parenting Game in order to be satisfied when the game is over and their children are grown up. The rules in these homes were often very similar, if not identical, to the rules in the families of disappointed parents.

Nonetheless, some characteristics of these parents, *taken as a whole*, are of particular interest:

- When most of these parents started their families, they discussed the values they wanted to pass on and how they planned to do it. High on their lists was spending time with children and letting them know they were loved. They did not believe financial "success," either theirs or their children's, to be nearly as important as "integrity."

- For many of the parents, extended family and church reinforced their values. Youth activities mitigated against drug use. One family deliberately moved away from a family-of-origin they perceived as problematic so they could develop a healthier support system elsewhere.

- Many parents in the survey came from families that were alcoholic, abusive, and neglectful. Although a few of these parents had therapy somewhere along the line, in the majority of cases a primary ingredient in helping them overcome difficult backgrounds seemed to be their determination to raise their children in a healthy environment. As one parent said, "We looked at what mistakes our parents made and simply decided we weren't going to make those same mistakes." Such an attitude certainly puts an interesting twist on the I-can't-help-being-dysfunctional-because-my-parents-were-dysfunctional trap into which some adult children have fallen.

- Parents did not give unsolicited advice to grown offspring. Typical was one mother who, when asked by a friend why she would agree to pay for her son's major in college (a liberal arts pursuit unlikely to lead to financial rewards), answered, "Could *you* make a decision for somebody else's life?"

- Some of the children of these satisfied parents were involved at one time with drugs and/or alcohol. Their parents' efforts to straighten out these children were not necessarily different from those of parents who were not successful in stopping their child's abuse. The main reason a child became clean and sober appeared to be the decision of the child that he *wanted* to be clean and sober. This doesn't mean that these children "just said no" to drugs. But being in a recovery program did not appear to be essential, although often it was helpful.

- Several expressed the view that God lends children to parents, who must do their best and then let God finish the job "with the cooperation" of the adult child.

- *The one characteristic that was shared by almost all of the satisfied parents was a father who was involved in family life to a much greater degree than were most fathers of that generation.* This was consistently true whether or not the parents were divorced. Somewhat untypical, however, was one father who, denied access to two children by his first wife, said he had "no feelings" about how they turned out. He feels neither guilty nor responsible for the fact that both of them have difficulty with jobs and relationships. On the other hand, he received custody of the two children from his second marriage and has a close and rewarding relationship with them, is aware of his feelings, and is able to communicate those feelings to his children. It is interesting to note that even when these satisfied fathers could not talk freely about *their* emotions, they communicated with their children about many things important in a *child's* world.

The Influence Ordinary Parents Have on Their Children

It is said that if you are satisfied with your sex life, your satisfaction with sex occupies 15 percent of your emotional energy. If you are dissatisfied with your sex life, your dissatisfaction occupies 85 percent of your energy.

A similar statement can probably be made about disappointed parents. When things turn out *pretty much as expected*, parents give little thought as to how much they have influenced the outcome. When things *don't turn out as expected*, parents often give a *great* deal of thought to the role they played. Eventually, most disappointed parents turn their attention and energy to other problems. In the meantime, they may wish they had a formula that could tell them how much they have been responsible for their child's situation. I have often wondered what percentage of David's problems *I* was responsible for and what percentage *he* was. Just how guilty should I feel?

Would things be different for David today IF I had insisted on family therapy when David was a teenager; IF I were less uptight and more easygoing; IF I hadn't gone back to work when he was seventeen; IF I had attended more than one of David's polo matches when he was goalie; IF I had been more aware of his need for praise; IF my own self-esteem had been higher; IF we had joined a church or other organization that could have reinforced our values; IF, IF, IF . . .

Although, as noted earlier, the source of much pain and suffering can be traced to parental abuse, evaluating the uneven parenting of average, imperfect parents is tricky. There is no proven, direct correlation between *specific* parenting decisions and the personalities and choices of children.

If it were possible to develop such a perfect formula, it would need to resemble the intricate, highly complicated designs of Rube Goldberg. The formula would probably begin with the number of times a parent attended back-to-school night, times the number of hugs to the third power, minus the number of times the parent failed to recognize the child's need for special attention, plus the number of times the parents expressed praise for work well done . . .

Acknowledging that my perspective is no more, or less, accurate than the theories of many others who analyze The Parenting Game, I have developed an "equation" concerning the various influences that go into making us the people we are. This observation is based upon my personal experience and that of my clients and upon information I gained in interviews with both satisfied and disappointed parents. Although arbitrary, when I've shared this formula with clients and colleagues they're agreed that it makes a lot of sense.

Except in cases of sexual, physical, and emotional abuse, in the great majority of families we can divide the influences on a child's life into three fairly equal categories:

- The decisions and personalities of both parents
- The child's physical and mental attributes, temperament, and choices
- A combination of the environment outside the home and circumstance

The Decisions and Personalities of Both Parents

It takes two to tango. It takes two to make a meaningful marriage. It takes two to parent. Although mothers have been conditioned to accept the lion's share of responsibility for child rearing, fathers and mothers provide different, complementary influences on how their children will function later in life. I believe that the influence most parents—note the plural—have over the way their children turn out is approximately one-third of all the factors that help create values and personalities.

This means that mothers, who are only half of the parents of each child, have contributed only *one-sixth* of all the influences on a child's life. If you are a mother who has been burdened with overwhelming guilt, notice what this view of parental influence can mean to you. You can take off a few layers of the guilt you've assumed is all yours and start looking at other factors that have helped shape your child, including your husband's one-sixth influence.

It is important to remember that even when a parent is partially, or totally, absent from the family through divorce, death, or desertion, the absence and lack of involvement of that parent is, in itself, an influence! The absent parent's influence on his children is based on the fact that they are deprived of his experience and his point of view—whether or not that view would be beneficial if shared.

Some single mothers will resent sharing "parental" influence for their child's success with a non-contributing father; they understandably want praise when things go well. They definitely deserve a great deal of credit for their efforts. And perhaps much of how well, or poorly, their child does can be traced to how they parented. However, single mothers, and those with inactive husbands, cannot do their job of parenting from a *female* perspective AND demonstrate what it means to be *masculine* at the same time. They can only give a woman's view of what they think a man's perspective is, or should be.

My limited survey of satisfied parents cannot be used as a statistically valid study for the relationship of a father's participation in child rearing and how likely the parents are to be satisfied in The Parenting Game outcome. Nevertheless, I am impressed with the fact that, as stated earlier, *almost all* the satisfied fathers I interviewed communicated more openly with their children than did the fathers in those families in which the parents were disappointed in how things turned out. Conversely, most, if not all, of the disappointed single mothers reported that their child's father was almost, or completely, noncontributing both in finances and time spent with the children.

I am drawn increasingly to the conclusion that fathers are a vitally important influence on "how children turn out." If mothers are to be held to a higher standard of responsibility than fathers, where is the mechanism by which they are supposed to overcome their partner's lack of involvement?

Fortunately for future generations, growing numbers of fathers are beginning to appreciate the importance of participation in the lives of their children. One man writing to Ann Landers said his relationship with his five-year-old son was "the best thing that ever happened to me, except maybe meeting his mother. I feel sorry for men who think working an extra day a week or running off with their buddies is more important than raising their children to be loving, compassionate people. When my little guy says, 'Daddy, you are my very best friend,' it is the highest compliment I will ever receive."

The Child's Physical and Mental Attributes, Temperament, and Choices

When we agonize over an adult child's situation, we rarely pay sufficient attention to the factors that nature, and our child's own temperament and choices, help determine. Nature may not be destiny, but it can surely steer the game in one direction rather than another.

Consider the following:

Gender

As millions of parents have discovered, the sex of a child is outside our control without scientific assistance from modern medicine. Yet gender *greatly* influences how that baby will experience much of life—experiences which encourage or discourage the achievement of equality in the future. Take school as one example. Studies indicate that boys get more attention from their teachers than do girls at all grade levels, be it praise, criticism, acceptance, or remediation. Curricula often ignore females or reinforce stereotypes. For example, a review of books that have won the Caldecott Medal (the "Pulitzer" of children's books) found ten boys depicted for every girl.

Physical attributes

Children considered good-looking tend to be the most popular. Tall children are assumed to be more intelligent. Rising above stereotypes that attribute advantages to those more favored by nature is possible, of course, and the process may even develop greater character. But it's not easy. Children born with disfiguring birthmarks or physical handicaps have limitations and challenges other children do not.

Mental characteristics

Today there is a great deal more hope for children with Downs syndrome than there was twenty years ago because we have learned how to take fuller advantage of the child's potential for greater mental achievement. Yet a child with Downs is not going to be a brain surgeon no matter how much intellectual stimulation parents and schools provide.

On the other hand, consider the case of five-year-old film (yes, five!) director Gregory Scott, who already has four films under his belt, a new five-year contract, and appearances on "Arsenio" and "Entertainment Tonight." He didn't reach this point in his short life because his mother pushed him. Gregory started talking at four months! At twelve months, when he was speaking in "big sentences," he saw his first movie, "The Aristocats," and left the theater singing one of the songs. By three-and-a-half he'd decided on film-making as a career.

Temperament

Every parent with more than one child knows that each baby responds to the world differently from the day he or she is born. What makes the child different, in large part, is the temperament or character traits that vary from person to person and seem to be a natural, inborn style of behavior, a style parents may work with or against but that is unlikely to change significantly. The following are a few words both satisfied and disappointed parents I interviewed used to describe *traits of their children that were consistent from earliest childhood through adulthood:* calm, self-assured, assertive, stubborn, self-reliant, competitive, very dominant, tenacious, independent, sweet and gentle, shy, rolls with the punches, bubbly and outgoing, introverted, moody.

Choices

Certainly the physical and mental characteristics of our child help determine how he is shaped by his environment. But something else comes into play. It is what I've coined the "child-environment feedback loop." The environment may act upon the child, but the child, through temperament and an inclination to respond in an idiosyncratic way, helps determine whether one environmental factor will be more influential than another. In other words, the mindset out of which our child's past choices were made will influence his current mindset and his future choices. The effect of his choices in shaping his world, and in what he therefore gets from the world, are not inconsequential. His own choices help determine how he will turn out.

Outlook on life

Finally, when we consider the way in which our child contributes to his own destiny, we observe something that goes beyond temperament and choice and yet is part of both of them. That is the basic outlook each person brings to life. We all know people who reach out and make the best of tough circumstances. They may be struck down by illness and catastrophe, assailed by grief and failure, treated unfairly or betrayed. They not only survive, they confront their stresses and sorrows in ways that deepen their lives. Happiness for them does not depend on outward circumstances.

If people have grace, distinction, and courage only because their parents taught them those qualities, how is it that many families have both defeatists and opportunists? Much seems to depend upon a special quality, or lack of quality, within each child.

A Combination of the Environment Outside the Home and Circumstance

When parents consider the issue of genetics versus environment, they tend to focus on the environment *inside* the home and not the environment *outside*, in the wider world. They fail to remember that the beliefs, values, and attitudes of parents are not created independently of the culture and times in which they live. The complex, ever-changing world outside the home has a complex, ever-changing influence on our children.

A few of the experiences our child has when he leaves our house can expand our appreciation for the many factors that impinge on our child's development. For instance:

- The indulged, narcissistic, and persistently adolescent baby boomer generation, fed by advertising and a prosperous economic climate, placed an inordinate emphasis on materialism, physical beauty, and fashion. This climate has exerted a strong influence on people's behavior and attitudes, just as the climate of the Great Depression and World War II affected parents in other ways.

- While World War II was followed by unprecedented prosperity, young adults today face a much more adverse economic climate created by a changing world market, excessive government debt, failed S&Ls, bankruptcies, and other factors far outside the control of parents.

- The average child spends over twelve thousand hours watching television before he is eighteen! He is given a distorted picture of life, served up by cop shows and family sitcoms in which every problem is easily solved in thirty minutes. These shows can all too readily be taken at face value by impressionable minds.

- Although disparate ethnic and racial groups may eventually meld into a rich and harmonious society, our very imperfect society today provides different children with different social experiences and opportunities.

- Relatives, peers, and neighbors offer experiences beyond what the immediate family can provide. My children, for example, did not have the advantage of an extended family nearby. However, they traveled through many states and have cruised Georgian Bay in Canada with their grandparents, opportunities most of their friends did not have.

- Inequalities in medical care create a society in which only some children have access to the best treatment. Most significantly, prenatal care is unavailable to *one-fourth* of America's pregnant women. Since babies born with health risks resulting from their mother's lack of medical attention have several strikes against them, they have been "influenced" by society long before they must challenge life in the world outside the womb.

- Our public education financing system allows one school in a Chicago suburb to draw upon $340,000 worth of taxable property for each child, while a school in the middle of Chicago must rely on property wealth worth one-fifth that amount.

There are hundreds of other ways our children are influenced by the environment outside the home, from gang violence to churches and civic groups working for change; from easy availability of alcohol, cigarettes, marijuana, and crack to amazing scientific breakthroughs; from an educational system that may fail to teach children how to locate Europe on a map to stimulating and informative documentaries.

To understand this one-third influence on our child's life, we need to look carefully at a significant factor and an intrinsic part of it: circumstance. Whether we believe that what happens to us is dictated by divine intervention (acts of God) or by happenstance (luck), circumstance is a decisive factor in determining how events shape our lives for good or ill.

Consider our first circumstance. Birth. The order in which we appear in our family has an intriguing ability to affect our personality. Only children, for instance, tend to be independent and achievement-oriented, with high self-esteem. Firstborns often are considerably more apprehensive and anxious. Yet their self-critical perfectionist traits can contribute to success: Half of our presidents have been either firstborns or firstborn sons and of the first twenty-three astronauts in space, twenty-one were firstborns. On the other hand, a middle child who usually learns from a relatively early age how to share and get along with others, is likely to be more easygoing and friendly. The youngest in birth order are more likely to be fun-loving than are older siblings.

Clearly the interactions of siblings, can greatly influence how each child develops. Consider the case of Tonia, born with a hip problem, who had a splint that prevented her from walking for two years. When she threw toys out of her playpen, her older siblings obligingly retrieved them. Her parents suspect that the availability of an audience (the consequence of Tonia's position as third child rather than firstborn) contributed to the fact that she has a "performer personality" and loves an audience.

Family events that affect everyone in the family do not affect all the children in the same way. Much will depend upon their ages and needs at the time a particular circumstance happens. A two-year-old boy will experience his parents' divorce differently from his older brothers, eight and twelve. A girl who might have become an Olympic gymnastic champion must give up that dream if her father loses his job and there is no free program for gymnastic lessons. Yet her sister who loves school and reading can still shine as a scholar and take advantage of free library books.

Circumstances within the environment, both inside and outside the home, definitely play a major role in the outcome of a person's life!

Parents with More than One-third Influence

Although the majority of parents can be said to contribute approximately a one-third influence toward how their children will turn out as adults, there is much greater effect upon a child when parents (1) abuse their children or knowingly tolerate the abuse of their children by others, (2) are alcohol or drug abusers, (3) stifle and suffocate their children in the name of love and protection, or (4) have serious mental illness.

Abusive Parents

It is fairly easy to recognize the characteristics of abuse when parents use children for sexual gratification (with or without penetration) or when corporal punishment is excessive (even when parents claim it is done "for the sake of not spoiling the child"). These offenses are not only harmful to children, they are criminal acts, although parents are seldom prosecuted because the privacy of a home provides protection against incriminating evidence and corroborating witnesses.

It is less clear as to what constitutes other kinds of abuse, especially physical abuse. A parent is obviously, and criminally, negligent if he locks a child in the shed in the backyard or deliberately starves his child. One can convincingly argue that a pregnant woman abuses her unborn child if she uses crack. And the daily newspaper all too frequently provides examples of real and frightening physical abuse.

Other examples can be trickier to evaluate. For example, is a father "abusive" if he smokes cigarettes and his child develops asthma? Or, to take a more extreme example, what if a mother frequently takes her children to McDonald's and they develop clogged arteries after years of eating fatty foods?

Accusations of emotional abuse, which underlie many confrontations parents find difficult to accept, are even more elusive. Yet we can draw a fairly clear distinction between the parent who firmly challenges his child in a supportive environment and a parent who has no regard for the child's growing sense of self nor her need for nurturance. The emotionally abusive parent responds to misbehavior with punishment that may not hurt physically but is clearly out of proportion to what the child did and far beyond anything needed in order for the child to learn a lesson.

In defining "abuse," the dictionary uses the words "wrong," "misuse," "mistreat," "excessive," and "insulting." In the narrowest use of the term, a mother who yells insults at her children after a hard day ("how could you be so stupid as to forget your homework?") abuses them by belittling their sense of self. If she later apologizes or rarely engages in such behavior, her children aren't going to suffer long-term damage. However, cruel, belittling insults delivered day in and day out are emotionally abusive and can damage the child's sense of self for the rest of his life.

Alcoholics and Chemically Abusing Parents

It is easy to see the difference between someone who can stop at one drink and another who always gets blasted. However, it's not easy to evaluate our behavior when the drinking is in the range of what might be moderate, slightly more than moderate, or sliding over into the characteristics of true abuse. For example, there is a fine line between using a little more alcohol than might be good for us (in which case we may periodically have a hangover) and drinking a bit more than that (in which case we may end up losing our license because we've driven under the influence). The same difficulty exists in evaluating the effect of mind-altering drugs like marijuana, cocaine, and Valium. However, some parents who abuse alcohol and/or drugs can sometimes effectively hide their abuse from their family, and their children will not show any significant effects from growing up in such homes.

So it is possible that even if you *were* an abuser of alcohol or drugs, your children may not have been affected to a great degree. However, it is more often the case that when one or both parents drink excessively or abuse a wide range of mind-altering chemicals, the environment in the home becomes unstable and chaotic. While such parents might not be prosecuted for abuse (alcoholism and drug abuse by themselves are not considered crimes), children in these families must develop coping mechanisms to survive in such an atmosphere. Based on their experience, they view chaos as normal. This skewed perspective frequently causes problems when they later attempt to form families of their own.

Controlling and Excessively Demanding Parents

Increasing attention is being given to families in which parents prevent their children from acting independently when they become adults because they never allow their children to function as separate individuals in the family. These parents find it incomprehensible to believe that their actions could have been damaging. They merely wanted the "best" for their offspring. They are seldom able to understand, when their child does find the courage to act independently and confront them, that children need breathing room in order to learn to make their own decisions. Skills in reasoning and self-confidence cannot grow when parents control, or try to control, every movement and decision of their children.

Mentally Ill Parents

Mental illness refers to certain thought patterns and behaviors that are significantly outside the norm of human behavior. We may think that any parent who is mentally ill would surely affect her child's life dramatically. Yet mental illness does not *automatically* prevent some people from being relatively good parents; in fact, many of them are as effective in parenting as those of us who would not be considered mentally ill. Nonetheless, I include mental illness as a possible condition in which parents can influence their child more than the average parent. As a twenty-seven-year-old client of mine will attest, while living with a schizophrenic mother is not necessarily an "abusive" situation, life is decidedly more difficult when a small child must be the intelligent, functioning member of the family; the effect her mother's illness has had on her life is significant.

✦　✧　✦

If you fit the description of any of the parents described above, you have had more influence on your child than the average parent. How great that influence has been will depend upon many factors, and I would not venture to give a percentage. However, I can tell you that coming to terms with your role in your child's life is possible, even though it will require courage.

Acknowledging that you may have harmed your child through mistakes you had not intended is essential. It places you in a good position to achieve genuine healing in your relationship with an adult child with whom you may be alienated or in whom you are somehow disappointed. You are far ahead of parents who have hurt their children and are unwilling to acknowledge that fact. Although you cannot change the past, it is not too late to develop a better relationship with your child in the future.

Please note: Just because you may have had a greater-than-average influence on your child's life, an influence that was not nearly as positive as you would have liked it to be, does not mean that your child must forever function under the weight of that experience. People can change; they can heal, as the next chapter points out.

Chapter 4

Letting Go: Easier Said Than Done

"Letting go" is a process in which we change our relationship to our children and transfer responsibility for decisions concerning their lives from us to them. If we successfully complete this transition, we will accept our children as independent individuals just as they are—including imperfections and conflicting values—and they will accept us in return. We will communicate openly and share our values and experiences with one another, without believing we have the right, or the power, to change the other person.

On the other hand, when disagreements between the generations cause conflict or when a major rift tears straight down the middle of our family, letting go with love is a thorny process indeed.

But there is good news for disappointed parents. Even in the most difficult of circumstances many parents have made the journey from disappointment to true acceptance. Encounters with their children are no longer reminders of how things *should* have been but aren't. Many enjoy genuine adult-to-adult relationships; others have experienced closure and peace when contact with their adult child is not possible.

The Path of Healing for Parents

Coming to terms with family conflict we had not expected requires courage, determination, and time. We need these qualities if we are to move through a process I call "The Path of Healing for Parents." Along the path are five stages, each of which involves certain tasks for the parent to master before he or she can move on to the next stage.

Stage 1: My child fails to meet my expectations

Stage 2: Trying to change my child

Stage 3: The Velcro syndrome

Stage 4: Releasing the past

Stage 5: Letting go and resolution

There is no direct, linear progression through these stages, but much overlapping, backsliding and stalling. A parent may skip quickly through one stage and then spend long months, even years, in the next. You will only give yourself more grief if you assume there is a "right" way to heal. Nevertheless, you can use the experience of others as an encouragement to take the steps needed toward finally letting go with love.

Stage 1: My child fails to meet my expectations
Task: Honestly acknowledging my disappointment

This first stage begins when parents realize that their child has not met their expectations. They feel disappointed. What they do with that disappointment, as pointed out in the second chapter, will depend on many factors.

Forming an adult-to-adult relationship

After observing that things haven't turned out the way they expected them to, some parents will move almost immediately to the fifth stage and let go with love. The situation in which these parents find themselves, plus their personalities and attitudes, create a climate in which an adult-to-adult relationship can grow.

Being disappointed does not mean you will *necessarily* feel guilty, have issues that keep you stuck in your disappointment, feel a need for forgiveness, or want to grieve what hasn't happened. You may accomplish the task of this stage—honestly acknowledging that you are disappointed—and then be able to let go. If you can do this, I suspect that your response is rare (and you probably don't need this book), but I do know parents for whom this has been possible.

Pretending everything is okay

Other parents may deny their disappointment and try to convince themselves that they have already let go, as did the mother in the television play discussed in chapter 2. But these parents *are* disappointed. They are just afraid to acknowledge it. They hide behind a not-very-concealing-veneer that implies parents must unconditionally accept their adult child's lifestyle and values, even if that lifestyle seems bizarre and the values expressed are contrary to their own.

We often take our cues for responding to a situation from others. Consequently, we may hesitate to voice a negative opinion if we think our spouse will disapprove of our position. For example, perhaps a mother believes her daughter deserves a partner with "refinement." She finds the brashness and unpolished manners of her daughter's husband very hard to accept, but her husband admires his openness and lack of hypocrisy. Afraid of being labeled a critical, interfering mother-in-law, she may say nothing. Over time she might even come to like her son-in-law and be able to let go of her disappointment that her daughter hadn't married someone else. In the meantime, her silence prevents her from getting the help she could use in resolving her discomfort more easily and directly.

Responding defensively or openly to accusations

Many parents think everything is perfectly fine between them and their child—until the day their child accuses them of being "dysfunctional" or "abusive" or otherwise claims their childhood was not the idyllic, or at least satisfying, experience the parents assumed it had been. Suddenly they are thrown into a state of pain and upheaval; their illusion of a contented family is shattered.

If this has been your experience, your child's comments cannot be ignored, unless you are willing to settle for a merely superficial relationship. Your son wants you to address old wounds that he believes have been swept under the rug. The wounds may be genuine scars from abuse you were unaware of causing, or they may result from the normal working-things-out process when adult children separate themselves from their parents. Whether the reality of your child's complaints are serious or relatively minor, the situation must be dealt with, or the opening rift in your family might tear everyone apart permanently.

Letting-go conditionally

Many parents do not realize they have placed conditions on letting go of their adult children. As far as *they* are concerned they *have* let go. In one way they have. However, when serious disagreements arrive on the scene, these parents often "take back" the letting go they had done earlier. Suddenly they are disappointed in something their child has chosen to do and may even feel betrayed, as though in accepting the parents' statement of freedom the child had agreed not to disappoint his parents.

It isn't surprising that such parents wonder what happened, how their child could end up so far from where they thought she was heading. Yet it often takes a long while for parents to realize that their children are not always going to please them. Different kinds of seedlings can look very similar when they first come out of the ground. It is not often possible to foresee the consequences of our children's decisions the first time they take a particular action or experiment with a philosophy. Just as we did, they find their way into adulthood with tentative steps and missteps. Parental sanity requires a wait-and-see attitude; otherwise, we might well fear that our children are *never* going to make it through adulthood.

When a short hiatus from college turns into a permanent break for our gifted child, we will be very disappointed. In the meantime, we keep expecting her to return, the sooner the better. Or consider the matter of deciding at what point the social drinking of our child has become a problem. It is often difficult to tell the difference between social drinking and addiction. Several years down the road, when we have had the benefit of hindsight, we may look back and recognize the beginning signs of our child's addiction. At the time, however, they are not so obvious.

Once parents realize they are disappointed, they usually do what I did—try to coerce their child into becoming the person they want him to be.

Stage 2: Trying to change my child
Task: Recognizing that my guilt, anger, and blame keep me engaged in unproductive efforts to change a child no longer under my control

We all know parents who attempt to mold their child's values and behavior *long* after the child has left home—often into middle-age and beyond. Maybe you, yourself, have parents like this and understand, all too painfully, the pressure of parents who won't give up. In such families there is no letting go, only hanging on.

If parents fear judgment because the "product" they have created is flawed, they may hope to avoid criticism by finding some way to correct those flaws. Evidence that their previous efforts were not successful only encourages their search for a better method.

Elinor Lenz, in her book *Once My Child, Now My Friend*, provides the following list of manipulative strategies parents use in their effort to "prop up the crumbling edifice of parenthood":

> Bribery: *"I might be able to manage that ski outfit you've been hankering for if you ——"*
>
> Appeal to guilt: *"And the doctor said it's all this stress I've been under ever since you ——"*
>
> Threat: *"As long as you're living under my roof, you'll ——"*
>
> Shaming: *"I should think you'd be more considerate ——"*
>
> Power play: *"You'll not see another cent from me as long as you ——"*
>
> Appeal from authority: *"I've lived longer than you. I know better, take it from me ——"*
>
> Unfavorable comparison: *"I don't understand why you can't hold on to a job and the Elmans' son, who doesn't even have a college degree, is a sales manager, and last year, his mother tells me, he made, with salary and bonus ——"*

Dire prediction: "If you go on this way, you know how you're going to end up? Well, let me tell you ——"

Invoking the dead: "It's a good thing your father/mother is no longer alive, because if he/she knew that you ——"

What is familiar is hard to change. And guilt is a very familiar feeling for most of us. In fact, it is the primary glue that keeps us stuck in this stage. Continuing our attempts to change our child is much easier than stopping our subtle, and not so subtle, manipulations. If we stop, we will forfeit our chance of ever getting a good parent badge. Continuing is easier than taking a hard, objective look at our situation, an analysis that might uncover how much we exacerbate and perpetuate the problem through our attitude and actions. Continuing is easier than moving on to the painful process of grieving for our lost expectations or forgiving ourselves and our child.

If our child preys on our sense of guilt to get what he wants, it is even harder to move out of this stage. The story of Barbara, a parent I interviewed, is a good illustration of this dynamic.

When Barbara's only child, Tom, was four and wouldn't share a toy with a neighbor boy, her husband, Frank, got violently angry and beat him so badly that he had welts on the area of his kidney. This very much frightened both Frank and Barbara. However, rather than getting help to learn better parenting skills, Frank withdrew from all parenting that involved discipline. Later, when Tom would complain about his upbringing, Barbara was the parent he blamed because she had become the sole disciplinarian, a role she was forced to take in the face of Frank's abdication of responsibility.

When Tom was eighteen, his father wanted a divorce so he could marry a younger woman. Angrily Tom told his father, "You will never see me again if you don't give the house to my mother." When Frank decided to give Barbara the house so she could sell it (which his father might have intended to do even without Tom's threat), Tom pressured her for some of the money. He saw his share as a retainer's fee, claiming "you wouldn't have gotten the house without my help." Although Barbara didn't agree with Tom's reasoning, she gave him $10,000, feeling responsible for not preventing the breakup of her marriage.

Today Tom, twenty-three, is much like his father, quick to get angry and lose his temper. Recently he had an argument with his girlfriend, broke up with her, drank some beers, and *rolled his truck in an accident. Barbara gave him $2,000 to pay for damages, even though she needed the money herself. Why? Tom did not need to say, "Mother, if it weren't for you, I wouldn't have had that accident." All he needed to do was to claim that he drank because he didn't know how to resolve an argument with his girlfriend: he knew his mother felt guilty because she was unable to resolve marital conflicts with his father. He simply implied that his mother hadn't taught him that couples can argue and still remain together.*

Fortunately or unfortunately for Tom, Barbara's new husband, Walt, can objectively observe Tom's appeal to his mother's guilt. Last year Tom wanted money to go into the construction business. At first Barbara was tempted, even though, again, she couldn't afford it. If she had been a "better" mother, she told her husband, Tom might have been more successful in school and today wouldn't have to struggle so hard to make a living. Walt helped Barbara resist Tom's efforts to play on her "failure" as a mother.

In the last chapter in the section on psychobabble, I talked about a parent who allowed a daughter to move back home, pointing out that he wasn't being "co-dependent" or "enabling," since she only planned on staying three months and since he could afford to help her. In the case just cited, however, when Barbara paid for Tom's accident, she prevented him from facing his responsibility in driving recklessly after drinking (even though he was not legally drunk). Furthermore, although his mother could not afford to give him money, she did so under the pressure of guilt. Money given out of guilt and/or the hope we can thus manipulate our child to become more responsible, more thoughtful, more respectful, is not money well spent.

Some parents keep trying to change their child not because of guilt but because, as discussed in the second chapter, they blame the child for causing pain in the family. Their anger prevents them from acknowledging how they, as parents, may have contributed to the disrupted relationship. Their angry pull on the rope across the rift is intended to demonstrate how much the family suffers from the child's intransigence. Unfortunately, such efforts almost never force the child to change, any more than do the efforts of parents who are motivated by guilt.

I spent a *long* time in this stage, probably half a dozen years, trying to get David to see things my way. Giving up guilt clearly did not happen overnight! However, when I finally acknowledged that the only thing I got from guilt was tension, some of the weight on my shoulders began to lift. The next stages required a lot of my time and effort, but as I approached those tasks on the road of healing, I could sense that I was moving closer to genuine peace of mind.

Stage 3: The Velcro syndrome
Task: Recognizing and dealing with those aspects in my own personality and outlook on life that keep me focused on my child, rather than on myself and my need to change

Through unrelenting effort a few parents are eventually able to get their "problem" child to behave and think in ways that reflect the parents' values. Or a child may change *in spite of her parents' pressure.* She may conclude that her previous lifestyle or choices were at the root of her problems, and her new decisions *may just happen to be* more closely aligned to those her parents find acceptable. In either of these cases the parents need not bother learning to let go. They've got what they wanted.

Most children who have not met our expectations, however, continue living as they wish, ignoring our good advice. This leaves us in a tough place. Rarely can parents sustain the effort to change a wayward child forever. Eventually we get rope burns from pulling that rope and we decide to stop.

Stopping, however, is seldom accomplished by moving directly from manipulation to letting go. Most of us have to first deal with the dynamic forces that have, until now, prevented us from letting go, forces that are more complicated than simple guilt and blame.

I call these forces "The Velcro Syndrome." As I see it, woven into the fabric of our lives are issues that we often ignore until they get caught (like one side of a piece of Velcro) with an adult child's similar issue (his piece of Velcro). If we learn to understand *how* we get enmeshed, there is a good chance we can avoid becoming caught in the future, or can extricate ourselves more easily when we periodically get entangled. More important, if we resolve our own issues, our unfinished business, we might more easily help our child resolve *his* issues when he asks for our help.

There are a multitude of ways in which we develop Velcro. The most common arise because of our insecurities: to the degree we believe our child's lack of self-assurance is the cause of her difficulties, we are reminded of our own. We grow Velcro when we insist that our beliefs are the only ones worth having and that individuals with conflicting opinions are just plain wrong. We may still resent the hurts from our own childhood; when our child tells us that *we* weren't perfect parents, we cringe. We had expected to do a better job and don't want to be reminded that we haven't been successful. Remembering the emotional pain we felt in being rejected by a sorority can come back to haunt us when our child is similarly rejected by a group. We may fear she wasn't "good enough," which is what we felt when we bought into the judgment of those we considered sophisticated.

This third stage is designed to help us see things as they really are, to better understand both *our role* and *our child's role* in the family tug-of-war. If our child feels entitled to affluence, are we hooked because we've worked hard for our success? When our child joins a fundamentalist church and tells us drinking is sinful, are we extraordinarily defensive because at times we secretly wonder if we drink too much? When our child chooses a partner we can't accept, do our prejudices unwittingly come into play? Does our child really lack a sense of social responsibility, or does she simply not share our need for constant involvement in community affairs? Is the resentment we feel toward our daughter justified when she tries to control family get-togethers, or do we overreact because we haven't dealt with our own tendency to manipulate others? When our son is taciturn and doesn't want to include us often in his life, are we particularly sensitive because that is a characteristic we found especially annoying in our ex-spouse and the reason we got divorced? Or is it possible our son doesn't share himself with us because we don't keep his confidences or because we use that information to criticize him for not living as we think he should?

The following nicely illustrates the Velcro syndrome.

> *Harriet, a single mother, came to see me because she was terribly upset over her twenty-three-year-old son, Paul. Every time she thought about his job as a short-order cook, she felt "wretched." Her obsession about him was affecting her performance at work. She claimed that "he's never been able to get his act together," and "has no ambition." It was not long before I realized that, while it is true Paul could be classified as an underachiever, his lack of motivation provided a mirror into which Harriet resisted looking.*
>
> *If she had been willing to look, she would have realized that she, too, is a very bright person in a dead-end job. Years ago she was distracted from the goal of attending college when the employer of her summer job after high school offered her full-time employment with excellent wages. She took the job without stopping to realize that, although the wages were good for someone with a high school diploma, they were not nearly*

*as much as she could eventually make with more education. As
the years went by, it was easier to work as a secretary than to
shift directions and start college. A boyfriend kept promising
marriage, even after Paul was born, but Harriet couldn't seem
to get him to the altar.*

*Not surprisingly, as Paul grew up his mother commented
on everything he did that was less than his potential. Soon
Paul discovered he had the power to get his mother's attention
by doing less than he was capable of. He played the role of un-
derachiever so well that he never developed skills or self-motivation to succeed.*

*When Harriet finally looked at her own underachieving
and enrolled in community college night courses, she was able
to get some distance from her focus on Paul. Whether her son
will ever work at his level of potential is no longer a significant
problem for her.*

Being objective concerning our child's situation goes a long way
in helping us untangle our Velcro issues. As the following story re-
veals, objectivity can also help us recognize the many ways in which
our child functions as an individual in the world outside our family.

*Mark, thirty-two, a lawyer, met a waitress in a restaurant he
frequented and moved in with her and her two young sons. His
parents, Stan and Evelyn, were already disappointed that he
had turned down an opportunity to work for a prestigious firm,
choosing instead to associate with a small group focusing on
low-paying environmental work. They were convinced they had
failed to teach Mark the importance of success. Now Mark was
"ruining" any chance for success by "living in sin," although
his parents were vague on exactly how that would happen in today's climate of greater acceptance for such arrangements. His
mother paid so much attention to how Mark wasn't living up to
their standards that she was sure Mark "would never make it."*

*Because of his parents' pressure, Mark wanted to stop vis-
iting them. But his girlfriend suggested he make an appoint-
ment to bring them with him to see me. She hoped that by
seeing a therapist uninvolved in the family's situation they
could accept him as he was and let go of their expectations that
he be the lawyer-son they wanted.*

*At first Stan and Evelyn were afraid I might take Mark's
side and criticize their standards. Instead, I assured them that
they could hold any standards they felt appropriate. Their only*

task was to see whether their expectations got in the way of seeing Mark as he really was.

In exploring how their focus on Mark's cohabiting might cloud their appreciation of Mark as a person, Stan and Evelyn made a list of values they wished to pass on to their children. They could see that Mark practiced many things on the list. He paid his bills, didn't use drugs or drink to excess, and was kind, generous, and honest. He called them periodically, although perhaps not quite as often as they would like. They realized that Mark had a positive influence on his girlfriend's children, something they were particularly proud of. By the time the inventory was finished, Mark's parents were ready to see him in a different light. Being the most successful lawyer in town no longer seemed so important to them, although they continued to view his living arrangement as "immoral."

Stan and Evelyn's moral grandstanding reflects their deeply held religious views. It does not make them toxic, dysfunctional, or abusive, only human. Their "Velcro" was simply the assumption that Mark's behavior outside the office, behavior *they* believe is sinful, is going to affect his success in the world. They did not need to give up *their* religious views in order to be more accepting of Mark. They only needed to realize that the world does not operate according to their standards, a realization that many of us have a hard time accepting. Perhaps the world *would* be better off living under a higher ethical code. Until it does, however, we can bend ourselves all out of shape when a child doesn't walk the straight and narrow as we define it.

Ignoring our own contribution to the family rift is like rowing upstream with one paddle. By the same token, acknowledging our own strengths—and human frailties—goes a long way in smoothing the rough edges of friction between generations. John, a man I knew several years ago, demonstrated this quality in an encounter with his daughter, approaching the problem in such a way that it didn't develop into a serious rift.

John raised his three children by himself after his wife abandoned the family eighteen years ago. At the end of a recent visit home, his oldest child, Valerie, said, "Dad, you were never there for me when I needed you. I was a nobody in a dysfunctional family." Then she abruptly walked out the door. Without assuming her comments accurately described a parental flaw, John reflected on the situation. He recognized that he had worked extremely hard to be the best parent he could, juggling

home and work; a reserved man, he knew he was more com-
fortable with his sons, who tended to be quiet, while Valerie ex-
pressed herself more dramatically. Yet John knew that he often
was there for her, although not always in the ways she may
have wanted.

John's ability to study the situation prevented Valerie's
comment from causing an unnecessary upheaval. When Valerie
visited a few weeks later, John calmly acknowledged that he
had probably missed giving her some needed emotional sup-
port. He apologized, saying, "I'm sorry I wasn't the kind of
mother you wanted." In return, she thanked him for his efforts,
as imperfect as they may have seemed at the time. In discussing
the matter further, Valerie realized that her image of a mother
was probably shaped by a few too many perfect TV families.

Again, this story reflects the complexity of parenting. Even
though we try our best, we are bound to miss the boat sometimes. If
John had tried to defend himself against the accusation that he was a
dysfunctional parent, he may not have been able to acknowledge that
Valerie needed the understanding a mother might have given.

I must have been covered with Velcro, for I got caught on almost
everything David said or did. As hard as I tried, I couldn't seem to
avoid getting upset. Discussions with him would result in one or both
of us feeling angry and misunderstood. I wanted him to change, although I knew there was nothing I could do. Yet *something* kept me
obsessing about the situation. Fortunately, I was motivated to discover what that something could be so that I could prevent myself
from reacting with pain every time we heard about David's continuing
chemical dependency, his loss of yet another job, his erratic behavior.

Chapter 6, The Velcro Syndrome, describes what I needed to do
to stop from getting caught in the rift with our son. My experience
may give you courage to address some of the issues that keep you
hooked in your child's situation.

Stage 4: Releasing the past
Task: Learning to grieve lost dreams and learning to forgive ourselves and others

As you work on the issues that cause you to get caught in your child's
problems, you will probably begin to notice some changes, however
small, in your relationship with your child. Great. Although the differences in opinions, values and lifestyles are still there, you've stopped
tugging on your end of the rope. Perhaps your child has stopped jerking on his end. You can facilitate this forward movement toward heal-

ing by choosing to work on the tasks of Stage Four, perhaps concurrently with your efforts in Stage Three.

When we view our family situation realistically, we may realize that at least a few of the differences between us and our children are highly resistant to change. In fact, they may *never* be resolved, no matter how thoroughly we work on *our* Velcro issues.

Our daughter marries someone we don't like. But because she is happy, we could wait forever to get a better son-in-law. Our unwed daughter decides to keep her baby. We have no power to make her give the child up for adoption, even though we are convinced that is the best course of action. Or even more painful, perhaps our daughter insists on adoption for a grandchild we want to remain in the family. And wanting our gay son to marry is almost surely a pipe dream, since few gays and lesbians (some professionals believe, none) can permanently change their sexual orientation, even if they would like to.

It is always possible that some of our expectations will be fulfilled *in the future*. In the meantime, we cause ourselves extra pain by desperately hoping things will turn around soon. If our son refuses to write or visit despite our best attempts to resolve old issues, we will need to wait until he works things out at his own pace. If our daughter's husband left her with five small children, it is unlikely she will soon return to college and get her graduate degree. My own son might eventually choose to enter a treatment program and develop a life that approximates the kind of future we once envisioned for him. Until that happens, I must accept what is true today. Otherwise, I end up back on the roller coaster of hope and disappointment that kept me in turmoil for so many years.

Whether or not there is a realistic possibility for future change, the reality is that we hurt today. Our child might become highly responsible five years down the road. That does not change the fact that he comes to us two or three times a year for bail-outs. Or our child may be willing to visit in the future, but currently refuses to see us. *Accepting the reality of our current situation, even if it seems to offer us nothing but pain and conflict, is a major step toward genuine letting go.*

In addition to grief, another catalyst for healing in this stage is forgiveness. Although forgiveness is an essential gift of the human spirit, we often fail to forgive simply because we don't know how to do it. It is easier than you may think.

Most of the parents interviewed for this book who had difficulties with an adult child said they had stopped trying to change their child and understood some of their Velcro issues. However, the majority agreed that grieving and forgiveness were areas they still needed to address more thoroughly.

This fourth stage can appear, at first, to be the most difficult of all; yet with courage to walk through it, it can also be the most rewarding. I will share some of my own experiences of grieving and forgiving later in the book.

Stage 5: Letting go and resolution
Task: Learning to develop an adult-to-adult relationship with our child, or bring closure to our relationship if reconciliation is not possible

Once we have uncovered our Velcro issues, accepted the reality of our loss of expectations, and forgiven those we hold responsible, we can really and truly let go with love. The letting-go behaviors we practice in this stage will no longer be a burden, something we do with gritted teeth because "good" parents are supposed to do those kinds of things. We can now experiment with different ways of letting go without the fear that unexamined habits and our heart's unresolved pain will unconsciously sabotage our good intentions.

Little needs to be said about this stage right now except that you, too, can let go with love. When you do, differences of values and lifestyles are no longer experienced as a "rift" but as the reality that parent and child do not need to agree in order to have a satisfying relationship. You *can* have peace within yourself and with your child.

Chapter 8 offers many practical ideas for making an adult-to-adult relationship really work. Chapter 9 deals with closure and healing when reconnection with your child is not possible.

Some Parents Let Go More Easily than Others

Many factors determine how easily disappointed parents move toward letting go, and how long they will stay in each particular stage.

A Premium Placed on Independence

Some parents actively encourage their children to be autonomous, to express their own points of view. These parents might still be very disappointed if a child makes what the parents consider to be serious errors in judgment or chooses an extremely different lifestyle. However, a more open attitude helps accelerate the process of full acceptance.

The Child's Situation Is Not Viewed as Serious

When a child's lifestyle is potentially life-threatening, as in alcoholism and drug abuse or in some cases of mental illness, it is far more difficult to disengage from Stage 2 than when differences between generations involve less serious problems. Nevertheless, even in those situations in which the possibility of permanent harm is not probable, some parents fear catastrophe looms around the corner.

They will insist on staying in Stage 2 so they can rescue their child at the first sign of danger. Other parents, in an identical situation, would be able to move on more easily to letting go.

A Support System Outside the Family

Parents, especially mothers, who have jobs, activities, and good support systems outside the home generally do not expend all their attention and energy in the raising of children. Contacts beyond the boundaries of the family expose parents to a broader perspective of life, including suggestions for solutions that might not occur to those who are more isolated. Mothers without that support tend to focus on solving the problems of their adult children. Since they have few other opportunities for their worth to be validated, they may hang on because they want proof of success in at least one area of life—parenting.

Success of Previous Life-cycle Changes

Life presents us with a series of opportunities, or life-cycle changes, when we must adjust to new realities: the birth of our first child, the entrance of that child into school, the day the child goes off to college or leaves home. How successfully we have negotiated earlier life-cycle changes is an indication of how easily we will move through the stages of letting go.

More than One Child in the Family

When parents are disappointed in the decisions and values of an only child, the struggle to let go is *much, much* harder. There aren't other children to whom the parents can point with pride and say, "Since *they* turned out well, perhaps I'm not such a bad parent after all." Parents with several children, of course, can also resist letting go of the one with whom they have conflicts. But their pain is generally softened somewhat by knowing their other children are doing okay.

A Solid Marital or Love Relationship

Paying attention to what an adult child is doing "wrong" offers an excellent distraction for spouses who have unresolved problems in their relationship. Because married couples are involved for many years in the raising of children, making a shift from parents to just-the-two-of-us takes adjustment in the best of families. Letting go of a child can be scary indeed if there is conflict in the relationship between mother and father (or between the unmarried parent and a significant other). This is especially true if the children were the only interest the parents had in common.

Willingness of Child to Disengage from Conflict with Parents

While parents need to stop trying to manipulate their child by pulling on their end of the rope, their children become responsible adults only when they, too, stop playing the game and get on with their lives. Adult children can make the letting-go process more difficult than it needs to be.

For example, Allison, thirty-two, wants to return home—for the fourth time. She claims it is just until she gets her feet on the ground again. Her parents don't have the courage to say no. Although Allison knows her parents wish she wouldn't keep coming back home, she plays a role in the family dissension when she fails to recognize that her inability to resist gratification is the primary reason for her frequent shortfalls when rent time rolls around.

Or consider the case of Philip, twenty-one, who knows he works below his potential in college. This is a constant source of conflict between him and his parents. When grades are discussed, his excuse is that he could do better if *only* he had not been forced to go to public schools, which he claims "stink." He thinks his mother should have taken a job to pay for private schooling when he was young. Although his parents thought it was more important to have his mother stay home, his harping on how they didn't care about a good education pulls them into a defense of their position.

When parents and adult children play the blame game, no one wins. And while it may seem to the participants that progress can be made through defenses and counter charges, the energy expended is wasted. Perhaps, if parents could purchase a two-way ticket that would allow them to return to any time in the past, they *might* choose to do things differently the second time around. Maybe not. But we can't go back in time. Blaming parents for making mistakes doesn't help parents understand how their mistakes were perceived by their children; blaming our children for the choices they are making as adults is equally fruitless.

The Path to Healing for Adult Children

"The Path of Healing for Parents" corresponds to another journey we might call "The Path of Healing for Adult Children." This is the process of healing broken parent/child relationships from the perspective of a grown child. This journey also has five stages.

Stage 1: Realizing my parents were far from perfect

Stage 2: Trying to get my parents to give me what I needed

Stage 3: Discovering how I get stuck in conflicts with my parents

Stage 4: Releasing the pain of childhood disappointments

Stage 5: Acceptance and resolution

Since this book does not deal with the adult child's perspective of family rifts, I won't discuss these stages in detail. However, they are presented here in a brief form because it is valuable for parents to realize that their children need to go through a healing process of their own; it helps to have some understanding of what that process involves.

Although the journey to healing for an adult child can be observed in individuals who have never been in therapy, the process is most easily seen in the therapeutic setting.

Many people enter therapy because they want to work specifically on conflicts with their parents. They know their parents weren't perfect and may clearly remember being abused. Often, however, clients come to therapy because their relationship is breaking up, they can't keep a job, or their children are having trouble at home or in school. They may hope to find relief from their problems if they could only get their partner to change, if their boss would just understand them, if their child would do his homework. As therapy progresses, however, they become aware that some of their attitudes and styles of relating contribute to their trouble with relationships, jobs, and children. These attitudes and styles of relating frequently developed out of their reaction to dynamics within families in which they grew up.

When these clients first began therapy, they might have portrayed their parents as wonderful, loving, kind, even perfect. Yet in the process of exploring connections between their childhood and their adulthood, they discover their parents' influence was not all positive but a combination of "good" and "bad," the result of uneven parenting. And if serious abuse was blocked from memory, it may slowly emerge into consciousness and must be addressed. So an evaluation of their childhood constitutes the first stage in healing.

Once the client focuses on his parent's imperfections, whether many or a few, he often gets in touch with some of his pain as a child. If there was serious abuse, the pain is multiplied many times. During this second stage, the client often tries to get his parents to apologize for the ways in which they failed to meet his needs, perhaps to make up for what he didn't get in childhood. Often, during this period, the attitude of children toward their parents is more negative than positive. This is when parents are frequently accused of being "dysfunctional," whether or not that term is used appropriately. The parents may wonder what happened to the compliant, apparently happy child they used to know. Yet the parents' willingness to recognize they were not perfect, to apologize if it is warranted, and to agree to work toward an adult-to-adult relationship will go a long way in helping their child.

Whether or not parents are willing to do these things, the task for the adult child in the third stage is to understand his own contribution to family conflicts. Disagreements are two-way streets. Just as he can see how his parents played a role in who he is, the client now begins to recognize the ways in which his behavior and his attitude toward his parents may not be the most healthy or effective if he wants a good relationship with them. Perhaps he plays on their guilt, expects them to rescue him from difficulties of his own making, or uses his imperfect childhood as an excuse for all his failings as an adult.

In the fourth stage, the client learns to let go of the unrealistic expectation that his parents should have been, or should be, perfect. He often needs to forgive his parents for what they were unable to give him. Surprisingly, this can even be possible in cases of severe abuse, although it takes a great deal of effort and time. In this stage therapy also involves letting go of the past by grieving for those times when his parents failed to meet important needs.

In the last stage, clients learn how to relate to their parents in more healthy ways than they have in the past. This can mean setting boundaries if their parents insist on running their lives or if they continue to be abusive. When clients move toward completion of the part of therapy that focuses on their relationship with their parents, they can learn to claim their rights and responsibilities as adults. They can learn how to make their relationship with their parents a more equitable one. If their parents are unable to have a healthy relationship or if there is no possibility for reconciliation, it may be necessary for the adult child to bring closure to the relationship.

Recognizing that our children need to go through their own stages of healing can help us in three important ways.

First, disappointed parents can gain a better understanding of their child by understanding themselves. We are all children of imperfect parents. While we have undoubtedly resolved some of the issues between us and our own parents, others may still need to be worked out. Nevertheless, *noticing that we have made progress in healing with our own parents helps us view the relationship with our child in a different, often more compassionate, light.* Our children need to come to terms with us and our imperfections, just as we have done and continue to do with our parents' imperfections.

Second, we can recognize that *the process of healing for adult children can take a long time, just as it can take a long time to come to terms with our disappointment in the choices they make.* Insights and steps forward are frequently followed by long periods spent digesting what is learned and trying on new behaviors. This shouldn't be surprising, since few significant changes in life are quick and easy.

Finally, awareness of this "Path of Healing for Adult Children" helps parents understand how their children may be working on one issue of the relationship while the parent is working on another. If our child has only recently begun seeing connections between his present behavior and his childhood, he may require time to sort out his role, and ours, in the family dynamics. Just because we have forgiven ourselves for not being perfect doesn't mean our child is ready to forgive us. *We may need to let go with love long before our child finds his own peace concerning us, his parents.*

PART TWO

Letting Go Leads to Peace

Chapter 5

Shifting Your Focus

By now you may be aware that old habits have kept your family conflict running on automatic pilot. You may realize that clinging to the hope that your child will eventually see things your way has kept you in the limbo of disappointed parents—unable either to let go with love or find peace for yourself.

Fortunately, three catalysts for change lie within easy reach: emotional pain created by the situation, the recognition that you alone are responsible for emotional reactions to choices your child makes, and the opportunity for personal change that naturally arises when children leave home.

Ten years ago the combination of these pressures forced me to stop my futile efforts to *change my son* and to start exploring ways *I* could change. Today, although my journey was long and sometimes rough, I wouldn't trade my struggles with anyone. My *entire* life (not just the part that involves my family) is much more peaceful than when I first decided to do something about the pain caused by my constant tugging on the rope (and David's pulling on the rope in response).

In learning to accept both the positive and negative ways in which I influenced my son, I developed a more objective, realistic perspective on life as a whole. In retrospect, I believe the situation with my son was a blessing in disguise. Even if things had turned out well for *all* my children, I needed to be a more balanced person, to avoid getting hooked by others and to let go of the need to control.

Pain: A Powerful Catalyst for Change

Family rifts are painful and hard to dismiss.

Unless we hide photographs of our child, every time we see pictures of her we can't help but reflect on how things have turned out. If family members are absent during holidays and birthdays, their *absence* pointedly reminds us of what *could* be but is not. If our child *does* come and arguments ensue, the day is ruined; we are thrown back into the pain of unpleasant family dynamics once again.

Events do not even have to involve our child for us to be reminded of the rift in the family. When we notice others in our child's situation, we are automatically reminded of our child's life, just as I think of my son whenever I see street people, even though he does not currently live on the streets. Conversely, we are made aware of unmet expectations when we see others doing what we think our child "should" be doing. Thus a gifted daughter's unwillingness to complete her education is brought painfully to mind when a friend casually mentions her child, a highly successful lawyer. The friend doesn't need to make a comparison. We make our own comparisons all too readily.

We may pretend in front of others that everything's okay. Within the privacy of our hearts we know the truth. Just as physical pain causes us to seek medical attention, emotional pain is an indication that *something* is wrong and needs to be fixed. But we can't fix our adult child. We can only fix ourselves.

Yet it is clear that many disappointed parents do not use their heartache as an agent for personal growth and change. Why are they reluctant or unwilling to look at the issues that keep them engaged in a futile game of who is right and wrong? The answer often lies in the dynamics of how pain arises and what we have been taught is the meaning of pain, as illustrated in the following stories.

Faye's only son, Mike, now twenty-six, was twelve when he decided to live with her ex-husband. Soon after moving in with his dad, Mike began to make excuses for not spending weekends with his mother when it was her turn to see him. Because Faye didn't want to be "a pushy mother," she accepted his increasing distance from her life without much protest. Now he sees her about once a year, although he lives in the same town. When asked how she feels about being excluded from Mike's life, Faye replies, "He's grown now. Why should he need me? Besides, I'm used to not having him around." She dismisses as coincidence the fact that migraine headaches always follow the few contacts she has with him.

Her case is typical of many in which emotional distress develops gradually. When Faye didn't insist on seeing Mike more often during his teen years, she became acclimated to a level of emotional pain she would not have tolerated if Mike had suddenly stopped visiting. Like the frog in the experiment who sits in a pan of water that heats very slowly until it boils to death, she allowed her pain to tighten its grip, bit by bit, unaware of how much she hurt—and by then she was too paralyzed to respond.

The case of Janet is almost the opposite of Faye's because Janet is very much aware of her pain. In fact, you could say that she wraps it around her like a blanket of martyrdom. Her attitude is a legacy from childhood when her mother accepted, uncomplainingly, frequent humiliation and even some physical abuse at the hands of her alcoholic father. Janet concluded that women must suffer to keep their families together. Furthermore, she has interpreted her church's message of sacrifice to mean she must ignore her own needs in the service of others. And so, although attempts at intervention have failed to stop her daughter's drug problems, she allows her daughter to continue living at home despite the emotional distress it creates for her and others in the family.

Gloria's church, on the other hand, preaches transcendence over emotional distress, claiming she can always be happy if she is willing to rise above her problems. Gloria believes that she, herself, set in motion everything that has happened to her, both good and bad, and she is afraid of "creating" trouble by speaking unfavorably of her son, who is divorcing his third wife. Consequently, she has become very good at pretending everything is okay. Whenever she talks about her son, she smiles sweetly and claims, in a tone that lacks conviction, that she doesn't "allow" herself to feel upset by his inability to maintain relationships.

These women share the illusion that they can find peace of mind by embracing martyrdom, by attempting false serenity through transcendence, or by rising above emotional pain even when the consequence is physical pain. These defenses may work for awhile; seldom are they effective in the long term. They are, however, prime examples of society's addiction to perfection, success, and omnipotence. We are so afraid of addressing our "failures" that we lose the opportunity they offer us for wisdom and an expanded capacity to embrace all of life.

Carol Pearson addresses the issue of personal growth that can arise from suffering in her excellent book of self exploration, *The Hero Within*:

Pain and loss are personally transformative not as a constant mode of life, but as part of an ongoing process whereby we give up what no longer serves us or those we love and move into the unknown. Each time we become aware that we are suffering, it is a signal that we are ready to move on and make changes in our lives. Our task, then, is to explore the suffering, to be aware of it, to claim fully that we indeed are hurting. But we can do that only if we have at least a glimmer of hope that our suffering is not necessary, that it can be alleviated, that it is not simply the human condition—or not simply our lot as a man or a woman. In this way, suffering is a gift. It captures our attention and signals that it is time for us to move, to learn new behaviors, to try new challenges.

When you are finally tired of trying to get your child to change, tired of family conflict, tired of getting hooked by every decision your child makes that you think is "stupid," you may finally yell "OUCH! Enough is enough!" Your suffering can then become a positive agent for change, even though you will be the one who changes, not your child.

Willingness to acknowledge your pain and suffering is an essential first step on the road to healing. But old habits die hard. Even after you begin your journey to letting go with love, you may sometimes find yourself again focusing upon your child rather than yourself. When that happens, just remember the pain that has brought you to this point. Say "OUCH!" and get back on track.

No One Can Force Us to be Happy or Sad

The second potential catalyst of change for disappointed parents is the acceptance of a simple fact of life. *Our child does not cause us to feel hurt, angry, guilty or happy—even when those emotions appear to be tied directly to our child's actions, values, and statements.*

Yes, when our child says or does something we consider harmful, immoral or irresponsible, we may well feel angry or experience other negative emotions. However, before we experience those emotions, we first process our child's actions and opinions through a filter. That filter consists of (1) the meanings we assign to various beliefs and actions and (2) memories of past events that were similar in some way to that of our child's current situation and that caused us problems we expect will also happen to our child.

Consequently, while it may appear that it is our child's supposedly "stupid decision" that has made us angry, we are only angry because *in our view of the world* that decision seems "stupid" and "wrong." We want our child to make another decision, one we consider "intelligent" and "right." It doesn't matter if three million people agree with us concerning what is harmful, immoral, or irresponsible—or if no one does. It is *our* beliefs that judge our child's opinions and trigger *our* feelings.

Imagine that your daughter Sally and her husband Jeff have informed you that they will not be coming to your house for Thanksgiving. Their decision is neither good nor bad, in and of itself. However, what you feel and how you act in reaction to their decision is not neutral. If they are going to Jeff's parents, *you may be hurt* if you believe Sally "should" spend Thanksgiving with you since she spent last Thanksgiving with Jeff's family. If Jeff's mother is confined to a wheelchair, *you may be pleased* that Sally thoughtfully offered to help in the kitchen, especially if you believe children "honor their parents" (and parents-in-law) by coming to their aid in times of need. However, if Sally and Jeff are going to the home of a friend, *you may feel particularly slighted* if you believe that holidays are meant for "family" and that Sally knows how you feel. How you respond emotionally to Sally's decision to spend Thanksgiving away from your house depends upon you, not her.

Many past conversations with my son perfectly illustrated how our beliefs and the emotional baggage of the past affect the present. When David wanted something I was unwilling to give him, I would often get upset while trying hard not to be. My old self-criticism tape was almost never disconnected. Listening to what it said, I would hear his statement as a criticism of me. In a way, of course, he *was* critical of the fact that I wouldn't give him something he wanted. But I heard his response as a criticism of me *as a person*, or as a judgment of me *as a mother*. Since I already had low self-esteem and tried so hard to be a good mother, it was the playing of the tape inside my head, not his words, that kept me hooked and in turmoil.

In addition to my critical tape, memories of my childhood and young adulthood would come back to haunt me when I observed David (or another of my adult children) doing something I thought particularly unwise. It would remind me of all the unwise things I had done in the past, things that could still cause me embarrassment whenever I thought of them. I wanted to protect my children from experiencing that kind of pain.

When David expressed an opinion that was particularly outrageous, I would feel my stomach tighten. If asked at the moment why I felt upset, I would probably reply that it was because I didn't want him to be considered foolish. But now I realize that I reacted as I did because I could see that his opinions were based on limited knowledge (yet how many opinions of young adults match the depth of experience of those who are older?). Again, I was reminded of myself. Too often in the past, unfortunately, I have said something *authoritatively* only to discover later that I was dead wrong. Being "wrong" was a big thing in my life, and I wanted my children to avoid that horrible fate.

Today, of course, I realize that getting upset whenever they made a decision I thought unwise was an acknowledgment that I didn't trust them to learn from the consequences of their choices. Besides, sometimes I didn't have all the facts, and their choices turned out to be exactly right after all.

There is no doubt that people can affect our mood. With certain friends we may feel upbeat and positive. Others who exude gloom and despair almost always drag us down. There *is* a relationship between our feelings and the moods and actions of others. However, when we insist that our child (or anyone else) *causes* us to be upset, we give tremendous power to our child (or others) to control our life. In the end, such a transfer of responsibility for our psychological health prevents us from discovering ways we can eliminate or decrease emotional turmoil when our child (or others) act in certain ways.

The first step in taking back control of our emotions is to say, "I allow my child to upset me." The second step is to say, "When my child does such- and-such, I let my attitude about that behavior pull me down." The third step is, "I want to understand what there is in my own experience that causes me to react to my child as I do."

Before we leave the issue of who is in control of our emotions, it is important to repeat the fact that we didn't deliberately set out to screw up our children's lives and make them miserable. So, too, *our children are not trying to make life difficult for themselves.* It is not likely that they are trying to make us miserable, either. However, if our child seems to enjoy seeing our distressed and negative reactions when he does or says something outlandish, that makes it all the more essential for us to disconnect our knee-jerk response to his provocation.

It is a moot point that we think our children *should* make other choices. They have been given the legal power to live their own lives, whether or not we like the results. And since we are the ones who get tied in knots when our child won't come to visit, drinks too much, spends money unwisely, or dates men we consider irresponsible, it is up to *us* to deal with our distress. Our child won't change simply because *we're* in pain. Relief will be achieved not through choices over which our child has control but through the discovery of changes we can make in our own attitudes and behaviors—*without discarding our basic values and beliefs.*

A Time for Different Windows, Different Views

At this point you may have said "OUCH" and agreed that you are responsible for your own emotions. You may also continue feeling stuck. What to do? Time to get a new perspective.

When my clients are unable to see options other than the ones they've always seen, I tell them that their problem is fairly simple. They need to look through different windows. I tell them that they have been living, psychologically, in a house with windows on every side. Like most people, however, they have only looked out of the windows that face in one, or possibly two, directions. By restricting their view of the world to what can be seen through their favorite window(s), after many years they assume that view is the "accurate" one.

No window's perspective is wrong—but each is limited. Because very few people look through all available windows, and because different people, especially those in different generations, tend to look in different directions, it is not surprising that parents and their children have different points of view, different perspectives on who is right and wrong, and different ideas on how to resolve conflicts.

After our children turn eighteen, we are given a perfect opportunity to look through new windows—and in so doing, to change our outlook on life, redefine our identities, and re-evaluate our commitments and relationships.

For starters, we must now adjust to a family organization in which we are no longer focused primarily on raising children. Many family constellations must change as boundaries expand to include in-laws and grandchildren. And while the "empty nest syndrome" may pose transitional problems for some, there is increased freedom and independence for us as couples (and for single parents as well). Errant children merely add another element to the changes we must make at this time of life.

Today's mother of grown children has almost limitless freedom to develop relationships with the world outside the home, if she has not already done so. She is free to create a different ending to life, a different identity for herself from that which was available for her mother and grandmothers. On the other hand, fathers who kept their eyes only on the ladder of success, power, and achievement may now want to take advantage of this period in their lives to confront previously ignored issues of identity, intimacy, and commitment.

This time of life clearly provides an ideal opportunity to begin a journey of self-discovery. It is an essential journey if we are to be vibrant individuals in the last decades of our lives, even if we don't have problems with our children. Only those who are hopelessly locked on automatic pilot don't feel some pull to reappraise their life about the time their fiftieth or sixtieth birthday nears.

Those who engage in a midlife realignment may choose to attend seminars designed for that purpose. For anything from a fairly modest to a substantial fee, participants can examine the manner in which they have constructed their lives. They can look through new windows as they are led through exercises to explore where they have come from and where they are going, what they see as the meaning of life, or their need for intimacy and compassion. Out of this examination can come a new script that, while riskier than the one they've been using, can rejuvenate their lives.

If nothing else, the combination of reaching middle age (or older) and finally having children past the age of eighteen provides a perfect opportunity for creating the respite for quiet reflection we desperately needed when our children were young. Remember those days? In addition to long hours at work, we washed sticky kitchen floors and walls at the height of our child's reach, fixed broken bikes, shopped for groceries and school clothes, reviewed homework, monitored sibling rivalries, read bedtime stories, searched for lost shoes. We longed for a place where we could get away from it all once in a while.

Now that our children are no longer constantly underfoot, we have increased leisure time. Even if our children are over eighteen and still living at home, there is probably some time we can take for ourselves. We can finally get away and concentrate on issues of personal growth.

Of course, "getting away" doesn't necessarily mean we need to go on vacations or expensive seminars. We can easily create our own retreat center by selecting a place in or near our house that offers the peace and calm we need to open new windows to the world. It may be a rocking chair in the living room, a patio in the back yard, or a quiet meadow in a park or woods nearby. If our retreat has comfortable, pleasant surroundings, we are more likely to use it. And the more we use it, the more likely we are to be successful in learning how to let go with love as we shift focus from our child to ourselves.

Here in this special, private place we can contemplate, meditate, read, and just *be* to our heart's content. There is no one around for us to impress. We don't need to *prove* ourselves to anyone; we need to *find* ourselves.

Choose Realistic Goals and Then Reinforce Them

There is no shortcut, no magical path to understanding and accepting ourselves as parents, or as people. Changing the relationship with your child will involve hard work, creativity, strength, patience—and the awareness that you are doing the best you can. I suggest you give yourself a pat on the back for accepting the challenge to learn how to let go with love.

As you begin this journey, you may discover very quickly that some of the pain and pressure you have been under for much too long is beginning to lift. That is probably because letting go of the rope stretched across the family rift (or at least refraining from pulling on the rope) allows you to use that energy for more productive ventures. Now you can make progress in resolving some of those conflicts over values and lifestyle that had previously kept you engaged in a fruitless game of trying to get your child to meet your expectations.

Achieving complete relief—and getting where you want to go— is most probable if you set your sights on a specific goal.

Consider how good it would feel not to feel discomfort any longer when you think of your child, to be completely responsible for your own reactions to what your child does or did; and to live at peace with yourself, accepting who you are and who you have been without recrimination or guilt.

There are other goals you might aim for as well. For example, if it would relieve tension between you and your son, might you be willing to visit your son's church—something you have so far refused to do because he says you are going to hell for not believing as he does, or because you say the same thing about him? Could you anticipate that arguments between you and your daughter might not occur so frequently if you simply decided not to comment on her lifestyle?

Remember that your goal can only focus on changes *you* want to make. It is *possible*, of course, that if you change the way you relate to your daughter, she will change in response to *your* change. In fact, it is *probable*. But *don't count on it.*

After all, your family is made up of individuals who've learned to relate with one another over a long period of time. In other words, your family is a system. And systems often resist change.

You and each member in your family, has a niche (or more likely several niches) where each of you fits. Primary bread winner. Arranger of family get-togethers. The only one who can get Granddad to calm down when he gets loud and bossy. The one who buys all the presents for the children or balances the checkbook or makes certain reservations are made for vacation trips. You may not *like* a particular role you play, but until someone (most probably you) makes an effort to change that role, you will likely be stuck with that position for a very long time.

What happens when someone decides to stop playing the role he or she had previously been assigned? Let me use our family as an example. I am extremely glad my husband is in charge of car mainte-nance. Since I am not mechanically minded and don't understand how cars work, a repair person could talk me into repairs I didn't need. But suppose Bob decided he was tired of taking care of the cars and announced that starting immediately I had to be responsible for my own car? At first I'd give him my best arguments, talk about my lack of aptitude and all of that. I would definitely plead with him to change his mind! If he *still* refused—and if I wanted to have a car that wasn't going to break down frequently—I would learn a heck of a lot more about motors than I currently know, or find a repair shop I completely trusted. I might grumble and complain, but I'd do it.

So it is very possible that if you decide to act differently toward your child, your child will make adjustments because of your new be-havior. For example, imagine that one of the problems you have with your son, Joe, is that you believe he is not very mature. There are many things that bug you about his lack of responsibility, but a fre-quently frustrating conflict arises over his late arrival to family events. Everyone knows he's going to be late, so they've gotten into the habit of arranging the dinner, or the highlight of the gathering, to accommo-date his late arrival. Every time that happens, you are reminded of his inconsideration of the needs of others. You get hot under the collar, but so far you haven't said much and what you have said has fallen on deaf ears.

Now, however, you decide to stop being controlled by Joe's per-petually late arrivals.

You begin by setting a specific goal for yourself. For instance, "I will not wait dinner until Joe arrives" or, "If we are leaving for Aunt Jane's and Joe has agreed to come with us, I will drive away from the house at the time we agreed to leave, even if Joe isn't there." What might Joe do in reaction to this new behavior of yours? He might com-plain that you are being overly demanding and aren't willing to be tol-erant of his easygoing approach to life—or he might start showing up earlier. *How he will change in reaction to the changes in your behavior is not under your control. Therefore, altering his behavior should not be a part of your goal statement.*

Establish your goal as something tangible. A real possibility. Not a vague hope that things will somehow get better. Although you may not be able to be as specific as the statements above, you can, never-theless, state your goal in terms that include your primary intention to act differently, such as, "I will remain calm when disagreeing with my son." Or your goal could be, "I will not ask my daughter to change her behavior, even though I strongly disagree with her lifestyle."

Of course, like New Year's resolutions that fade with the last notes of Old Lang Syne, the pressure of old habits can erode your intention to change. One way to prevent this from happening is to write your goal on several pieces of paper. Carry your goal with you in your wallet, put it on the refrigerator, stand it against a picture on your bedroom dresser, tape it to the dashboard of your car. These simple slips of paper can remind you daily that you've decided to stop pulling the rope and build some bridges instead.

Another way you can reinforce your intention to reach your goal is to do a very simple exercise. Stand at one end of a long room. Imagine you can see yourself, *as you will be after you've made the changes you want to make*, near the wall opposite you. Create an image of yourself feeling calm and serene. You may also want to picture your child standing near you, doing what he generally does that causes you to reach for the rope. Now imagine that you can be near him without getting hooked.

In other words, imagine that you have worked on the Velcro issues that previously would have caused you to react negatively and that you can now be near him, or think of him, without that automatic negative response. Be careful that you do not picture your child as having significantly changed his or her behavior, for that is something that may or may not happen.

As the exercise continues, you will walk four times across the room toward the image of your goal. Each time—keeping firmly in mind the image of what your life will be like in the future—you will say, preferably out loud, something slightly different. As you move closer each time to your projected goal, and as you use different words, you will likely notice a shift in your body—a shift not unlike what your body experiences when you hear someone express different degrees of affection in the statements, "I guess you're okay," "I think you're really okay," "I like you," and "I love you."

- The first time you move slowly toward your goal's image, say, "I *wish* I could reach my goal of remaining calm when my son disagrees with me (or whatever your specific goal is). Or, I *hope* I can reach my goal of . . . ." Stop every step or two and repeat the statement.
- Come back to where you started and again slowly move toward your goal's image. This time say, "I *must* reach my goal of . . . ."
- The third time you repeat the process while saying, "I *want* to reach my goal of . . . ."
- And the last time you say, "I *will* reach my goal of . . . ."

This exercise is designed to help you discover that *wishing* and *hoping* are passive and have little power to effect change. Thinking you *must* or *should* do something is also without significant impact because such directives have their origin outside ourselves: you can only be successful, in the long run, if motivation is internal. And although *wanting to change* is a more powerful desire than the first two positions, it is still not as potent as declaring *you will change*.

Honesty is the Best Policy

In a world of perfection, power, and status, there are many individuals—parents and non-parents alike—who fear having their "failings" exposed, even to themselves. Others do not view themselves objectively for the opposite reason: their better side is hidden behind a veil of self-recrimination, low self-esteem, and guilt. The greatest tragedy in both these cases is not the failure to achieve an ideal but the failure to live life fully, enthusiastically, looking through all the windows available and opening oneself to learning the lessons of life.

Our defenses of clinging to perfection or failure are protections against those things we are afraid to face, including the inner dragons that imprison us in the limbo of disappointed parents. But the dragons that guard the path leading away from family conflict and into healing are strange critters. They can be stared down and defeated by the truly brave. And the truly brave are those who are willing to see themselves as they really are, with all their strengths and limitations!

When we accept the challenge to be honest and to stop paying attention to whether we are "better" or "worse" than our ideal, we can discover a powerful dynamic of healing. By permitting others to see our shortcomings and vulnerabilities, we allow them to accept us as we *really* are. In fact, our limitations make it more likely that others will warmly accept us. After all, it is hard to feel close to people who seem "perfect." And being accepted, being liked, is what we all basically desire.

The value of this perspective for disappointed parents is very simple: *discovering we are loved despite our limitations, we can find it easier to accept the shortcomings of others (including our children)*.

In the privacy of your retreat, you can openly—and honestly—explore who you are at your best and at your worst, how you have changed over the years, and how you want to change now. Without pretense or defense, you can reflect on the goals you had for your children, how you attempted to shape their lives, how you were most effective as a parent, what you did least effectively. And you can begin to discover the Velcro that has entangled you unnecessarily in the details of your child's life.

A Support System is Helpful, if Not Essential

When you have been engaged for a long time pulling on a rope and staring at the child on the other end, it is not easy to stop pulling and shift your focus away from your child. Even if your goals are clearly stated, you will need a strong support system behind you. This added strength is necessary not because you are weak but because old habits die hard. Besides, there's no reason why you should have to make this transition by yourself. If you already have people in your life on whom you can rely, well and good. If not, now is the time to seek out those people who can give you a nudge when you start to backslide into old habits.

Tell these people that you plan to stop whistling the old tune of here-we-go-again-with-this-old-family-argument. Tell them that you plan, instead, to sing a song that opens your heart to joy and peace. Informing others of your intentions sends a powerful message to them and to yourself. They and you will know that you are no longer willing to live your life controlled by the choices of an adult child. They and you will know that you do not intend to expend any more time on energy-depleting family conflict.

Family members often have a vested interest in how things turn out. For that reason they can be a strong, positive force reinforcing your intention to change. However, they can also sabotage your efforts if they want you to continue playing a role, such as martyr-rescuer, for reasons of their own. In that case you may need to rely more on friends. Friends can almost always view the situation more dispassionately. Listening emphatically, they can notice when you begin to hum your old monotonous tune and can encourage you to sing another song.

In addition to the support you receive from family and friends, there are others who can also play an important role in your determination to change. You can get a new perspective and encouragement from professionals trained to work with family issues, as well as from paraprofessionals who have not had extensive training but who, nevertheless, can be exactly the person you need in your corner. Whom you choose will depend on how much you can afford and on what you need.

Official letters, such as M.F.C.C., that follow a name are designed to convey information concerning titles, licenses and training. Understanding what some of them mean can help you become a wise mental health consumer. For example, if there is an M.D. *and* Ph.D. after a name, the person is a psychiatrist and able to write prescriptions for drugs to counter depression and anxiety. When there is only a Ph.D. after the name, that person cannot dispense medicine and may or may not be licensed as a clinical psychologist. Both licensed clinical social workers (with L.C.S.W. or L.S.W. after the name) and marriage and family therapists (who are licensed as M.F.C.C.s in many states) must have at least an M.A. and often have earned a Ph.D. It is prudent to check with your state board to verify that the person you want to see is qualified and has a current license.

Paraprofessional counselors at your local mental health center may not have attended graduate school, but they have received training in crisis counseling and in empathic listening. Many priests, ministers, and rabbis have had some training in family systems and can offer encouragement and excellent support. Even hairdressers and bartenders can provide an opportunity to air your problems, helping you see you are not alone. With such help you may discover new insights into your situation. And there are many support groups for men and women working through personal issues; the group does not have to be designed specifically for disappointed parents.

Remember that the quality of the person (or members in a group) you choose to assist you in your efforts to change cannot be judged by how much training they have had or how much or how little they charge. *Generally*, the more training the better, but it's not an absolute rule. You will know whether someone is right for you if she teaches you how to be more assertive, if she encourages you to look through new windows that your family and friends may not have thought about, if she guides you toward new behaviors, if she helps you become unstuck from tight places.

You should be aware that the people who might help you can themselves sometimes get tangled in what are called "counter-transference" issues. In other words, their own attitudes and unfinished family business can get in the way of their ability to view your situation objectively. For example, your therapist (or minister or hairdresser or fellow group member) may imply, in not-too-subtle words, that you should take responsibility for your son's current problems. Perhaps he cannot see your parenting as only one of the factors that influenced your child's life because he is still very angry at his parents for mistakes *they* made. Remember that you deserve to be judged on the merits of your own case. Or the person working with you may short-circuit your healing process by trying to rush you through the grief you need to experience. Perhaps this person is unable to tolerate the pain you feel in being alienated from *your* daughter because she is afraid that she is losing a struggle she has with *her own* adult child.

I am not suggesting that professionals and paraprofessionals need to be anywhere close to perfect to be highly effective agents for change for disappointed parents. They do, however, either have to have their own family issues worked through to a significant degree or be able to set aside those issues when they are with their clients. You probably won't be able to recognize when the person you have asked for help is caught in a counter- transference issue. You will, however, be able to know whether or not you feel supported and understood by that person. If you can't develop a comfortable, trusting relationship with that person, for whatever reason, find another person or another group that suits you better.

Nevertheless, keep in mind that therapy is not a weekly ego massage to make you feel good. The purpose of reaching out for support is to help you become unstuck, to move on to what *you need to be doing* with your life rather than noticing *how well your adult child is doing*. You won't be able to accomplish that goal if you want a therapist or group who only agrees with you. We all need gentle, sometimes firm, nudges to help us change ourselves and resolve family conflicts.

Surround yourself with people who believe you can change and who encourage your efforts to make that change.

Chapter 6

The Velcro Syndrome

A letter that appeared in an Ann Landers column illustrates how parents and their children can become involved in the strangest kinds of disagreements.

> DEAR ANN: I realize that many people have problems that are much more serious than this one, but I'm so upset I just had to write to you. If I am too sensitive, please say so.
>
> Several years ago, my first grandchild was born on my birthday. What greater gift could anyone receive than the birth of a healthy, beautiful granddaughter!
>
> Unfortunately, this seems to have upset my daughter and son-in-law. They feel that their child should not have to share her special day with anyone. My birthday has never been mentioned since.
>
> Several days ago, I was with my daughter and son-in-law on my granddaughter's birthday. I kissed her and wished her a happy birthday. I then told her that it was my birthday, too.
>
> This angered my son-in-law. He abruptly turned around and walked away. My daughter became as cold as ice.
>
> Ann, was I out of line? Did I diminish my granddaughter's day by mentioning that it was my birthday also? If I'm in the wrong, I will apologize. Please give me your opinion.
>
> A GRANNY IN NEW YORK

> DEAR NEW YORK: Apologize? What for? You were born first.
>
> Your daughter and her husband sound like a couple of spoiled brats. Since they obviously feel that you are horning in on their child's birthday, I suggest that you manage to be somewhere else on that day from now on.

If "Granny" was unsuccessful in talking with her daughter and son-in-law, which would be the most direct route to resolve the situation, then it makes sense to suggest she spend her birthday with friends or other members of the family. Having a daughter who refused to acknowledge her birthday is, of course, disappointing. Nonetheless, the problem may simply be one of those glitches that happen when people with different ideas are in relationship with one another.

However, the birthday conflict could turn into a "Velcro issue" if Granny is so upset that she decides not to see her daughter any more (major ruptures are caused by smaller disagreements than this). And if she stirs up a hornets' nest by forcing relatives to choose between her and her daughter, she can turn an unpleasant situation into a horrendous family conflict. Then the only way out of the mess may be for her to explore *why* she has allowed her daughter and son-in-law to influence her happiness to such a great degree.

What is a "Velcro issue?" A Velcro issue is one in which a parent reacts intensely to her adult child's opinions or lifestyle either because of unexamined or unfinished business in her own life or because it is difficult for her to allow her child to make choices and express values that are significantly different from hers.

Not every parent who remains focused on her child has a Velcro issue. In some cases the parents primarily need to move on to the next stage and deal with grief and forgiveness. However, since we are all imperfect beings, we all have areas in our lives in which we are blind to our shortcomings or hold opinions that are unreasonable or insensitive to others. These imperfections are the "Velcro" of our personalities. They don't often bother us unless someone else, exposing his own Velcro, passes through our lives. Then we get hooked. Unfortunately, some of these people happen to be our children.

Interestingly, there is an important characteristic of this sticky stuff we carry around with us: a little piece can get caught almost as quickly as a large piece. Fortunately, it can also be removed more easily. The more diligently we work to remove our Velcro (the primary task of this third stage on the disappointed parent's path to healing), the easier it will be to avoid getting caught in a tug-of-war.

Although there are hundreds, perhaps thousands, of ways parents can get stuck, I have presented a few of the more common issues. They are not listed in any particular order of importance. However, I begin with perfectionism and self-esteem, since the combination of the two is a very common source of Velcro.

High Standards for Us—And for Others

When David first began using marijuana in high school, I would have described my self-esteem as a five on a scale of one to ten. Although I had already begun to work on my perfectionism, an outlook on life driven by the belief that I wasn't "good enough," I still had a long way to go. And as David's alcohol and chemical use continued and as he expressed a lifestyle and values that were very different from mine, I believed that he, too, was not "good enough." I *wanted* to accept him as he was, although I didn't believe that meant I had to approve of his drinking and drug use. I wanted to let him go freely, to stop my constant focus on what he did, or did not do, that society might, or might not, approve of. I wanted to have conversations that didn't end in arguments and disappointment for both of us. Somehow I couldn't. My low self-esteem kept getting in the way.

Perfectionists aren't the only ones with low self-esteem. However, since I am intimately acquainted with the dynamics of perfectionism, let me describe how this personality style develops a great deal of Velcro and how that Velcro gets hooked in many situations, not just with our children.

As the name implies, perfectionists are driven by extremely high standards. Wanting to do something well is not, in and of itself, a bad thing! It is just that perfectionists are caught between two polarities: omnipotence and impotence. No shades of gray. Only black and white. If they achieve their high goals, they can look down upon lesser achievers (which they imagine is almost everybody else) and feel on top of the world. Unfortunately, since perfectionists have limitations common to all humans, they are not often able to reach the high goals to which they aspire. What happens then? Generally they will feel like complete failures, *worse* than almost everyone else. It's a life with all the enthusiasm of an elevator ride, up and down, over and over again.

Not surprisingly, when perfectionists get tired of their need for perfection, they resent other people for setting the standards they've struggled to reach. What they fail to recognize, however, is that they, themselves, have chosen those standards—although, admittedly, their pattern for high achievement was laid down by others during their childhood. Nevertheless, they are unable to express resentment toward others; what would people think if they got angry? Instead, they turn their anger onto themselves, in the form of guilt, and onto others, in the form of judgment that others are inferior. How are others inferior? By not striving for, or achieving, the high standards they *could* achieve if they would only try.

Is this a portrait of what your inner life is like? It was mine for many years and I found it very burdensome. Now I see that *my perfectionism became my Velcro because I was stuck in believing that I was not the perfect mother (as I was supposed to be) as long as David had problems.* The idea of "uneven parenting" was not yet a concept I was able to accept. I even criticized myself for not changing rapidly enough. A *better* person would have been able to turn her personality around with less effort. And *someone else* would have handled disappointment in an adult child better than I did.

Fortunately, I kept plugging away at changing myself, and friends and colleagues encouraged my small successes. Eventually I was able to accept somewhat lower standards. In fact, I remember the day I first felt that I could be victorious over my perfectionism. I was in a grocery store and inadvertently knocked over a few small boxes. I decided not to pick them up. "Let the clerks do that," I said to myself. Now this may seem to you like a silly "victory." Perhaps you even think I *should* have stopped to straighten the shelf. For me, however, it was significant that I could be less than perfect and still feel I could be okay.

The opinions, values, and standards of others are, of course, important components in the development of a positive self-identity. However, I have learned, finally, to trust *my own* judgment as well—and to make sure that judgment is not too harsh. My willingness to set lower standards for myself has not only made my life easier, it has allowed me to do something I've needed to do for a long time—comfortably admit that I don't know everything. I can now ask questions without fear of being seen as incompetent.

Although I'm not yet as much of a non-perfectionist as I would like, I've come a long way. Nevertheless, I am convinced that my willingness to accept my perfectionism as a Velcro issue has been a major factor in helping me heal my pain and really let go with love. And although I suspect that David's situation has its roots in a lack of self-esteem, he must find his own path to achieving the self-esteem he needs.

Looking at Life Through Guilt-Tinted Glasses

A second cousin to perfectionism is the Velcro condition experienced by those who have a high "guilt-quotient."

Almost any of us can get stuck in trying to change our child because we feel guilty about this or that parenting mistake that might have contributed to our child's situation. For many parents, however, their guilt is not confined to their child. They feel guilty about almost *everything* they do. Unlike the Midas touch that leaves gold in its path, this personality characteristic leaves a trail of apologies and bad feelings wherever it goes. It's not surprising that such parents find it difficult to let go. And adult children discover that their parent's guilt is a particularly sticky substance allowing them little room to maneuver.

If you have tendencies toward the creation of guilt Velcro, you might want to see whether you can discover yourself in a list of "Twenty-One Characteristics of Unhealthy Guilt" compiled by Joan Borysenko, Ph.D., President of Mind/Body Health Sciences. As the title of her list implies, some kinds of guilt can be healthy. Our conscience *should* bother us when we cheat on our income tax, skip out on a debt, or lie to a friend. In fact, our society would be better off if some people developed a little more healthy guilt. But that's not the kind of guilt that creates Velcro for parents.

There is not, of course, an actual "guilt-quotient," based on the number of characteristics on the list with which you identify, that determines the volume of your unhealthy guilt. However, if you get to the end of the list with a sinking feeling in the pit of your stomach that Borysenko peeked into your psyche when she drew the list up, your task in this third stage of healing is to remove your guilt-tinted glasses and begin to see the world through more objective, clearer lenses. Fortunately, there are dozens of books that can help you deal with this trait, a trait that not only interferes with letting go of your child but also makes life much less joyful than it can be. (Dealing with guilt, incidentally, is where a therapist can be particularly helpful.)

1. I really know how to worry.
2. I'm overcommitted.
3. I'm a compulsive helper.
4. I'm always apologizing for myself.
5. I often wake up feeling anxious or have periods when I am anxious for days or weeks.
6. I'm always blaming myself.
7. I worry about what other people think of me.
8. I hate it when people are angry with me.
9. I'm not as good as people think I am. I just have everybody fooled.
10. I'm a doormat.
11. I never have any time for myself.
12. I worry that other people are better than I am.

13. "Must" and "should" are my favorite words.

14. I can't stand criticism.

15. I'm a perfectionist.

16. I worry about being selfish.

17. I hate to take any assistance or to ask for help.

18. I can't take compliments.

19. I sometimes worry that I am being, or will be, punished for my sins.

20. I worry about my body a lot.

21. I can't say no.

The "Right" Way to Live

We may consider it silly that our friend complains because her daughter-in-law sets the table differently than she does. At the same time, we can create a tempest in a teapot over behaviors and opinions of our adult children (or their spouses and children) that seem perfectly natural and acceptable to our friends.

We may insist that Republicans, or Democrats, will be the death of America and can't imagine why our son could possibly vote for one of "them." We may consider people who watch sporting events to be stupid dolts wasting time they could spend on more "productive" activity. Consequently, every time we see our son or son-in-law in front of the TV, we are convinced he'll never amount to anything.

Inflating our opinions to a level of "rightness," even "righteousness," they don't deserve, we create our own disappointment and distress far out of proportion to the significance of our child's situation. *The tenacity with which we hold our views as correct and others as wrong becomes what we might call "the Velcro of opinions."*

Differences between billions of people on the earth contribute to a kaleidoscopic world in which there are colors both brilliant and subtle and textures rough and smooth, harsh and soft. Yet there are many—too many, considering all the conflicts around the globe—who have difficulty thinking in any color but black and white. For these individuals the world is one-dimensional. And when such people are the parents of adult children who view the world in other colors, or at least in shades of gray, conflict is bound to ensue.

The following are some of the reasons we can insist that *our* opinions (and the behaviors based on those views) are "right" and the people who hold firmly to different opinions are "wrong" and "stubborn."

We Have Been Carefully Taught

We are born with no real sense of right and wrong, except perhaps an inborn fear of loud noises (which may be experienced as a wrong) and the need to survive (a right). Yet we soon acquire a long list of behaviors, opinions and attitudes that *feel* right to us simply because they are familiar and connected with comfort and love. Little things we learn in the home, like which way the toilet paper hangs from the roller or whether the glasses in the cupboard stand upright or upside down, are things that we take for granted as *right*, or at least *best*.

However, society also shapes our idea of what is right. Our ideals of beauty, for example, are arbitrarily defined by media and advertising, and we unconsciously accept these standards without realizing that we have allowed someone else to determine what face or figure will appear more attractive to us than another. Indeed, not long ago beauty contests actually defined the precise measurements of the "perfect" woman!

As a consequence of such nonsense, women have a great deal of difficulty accepting their naturally beautiful bodies. Few women, according to studies, can look in a mirror without focusing on all the things they'd like to change. With such an emphasis on looks, it isn't surprising that we develop lots of Velcro over *how our children look*. If our child is very much overweight or has some "flaw" that can't be hidden, we can try unceasingly to change that "defect" so that our child won't be seen as different, or less than normal.

The Fear of Being "Odd"

Having "normal" children. That is certainly the hope of most parents, although we may think a little individualism is okay and even to be admired. But there are not many of us who aren't at least a little concerned when our child has a characteristic, or holds an opinion, that definitely does not fit the acceptable standards of the group to which we belong, or to which she wants to belong. We want her to be seen as fairly normal, to fit in, to be accepted.

Understanding our own desire to be normal can help us deal with the concern that our child is not. Often, after I have worked over a long period of time with a client who has no psychosis or mental illness (but is in therapy merely to deal with the ordinary struggles that normal people often have), the client will, with some embarrassment, tell me about something he does or thinks that he considers terribly strange or weird. I am never surprised, for within nearly all of us there is something we keep hidden, something that we are sure others would consider "crazy" or "odd." It may not be a major concern for us, but we are nonetheless aware that we may be "different."

So it is not surprising if sometimes we wonder if our child really *is* crazy, or simply odd, when he expresses opinions or acts in ways that are considered abnormal by the average person. Maybe he is, if we insist on labels and our child fits the characteristics of mental illness as defined by psychiatrists. But often our fear that our *child's* behavior is dangerously out of the ordinary is fed by our inability or unwillingness to come to terms with the secrets that we fear make *us* different. Consequently, we can be very disturbed when we interpret some of our son's characteristics and opinions as not only different than ours, but weird as well.

When parents have a hang-up about what is or is not normal, *any* evidence of what they think is abnormal in their adult child (or in anyone else for that matter) can be extremely unsettling. For example, if such a parent has difficulty accepting a child whose sexual orientation is toward members of his own sex, the fact that she sees that behavior as aberrant, sick, or crazy will be the sticking point in the family rift. She will have to deal with her discomfort before she can let go with love. This does not mean she must view her son's behavior as perfectly normal. (If by "normal," we appeal to averages, it is not!) But she will need to understand what is so frightening to her about behavior that is not practiced by the "average" person.

What Will Others Say?

On the other hand, you may be a parent of a gay or lesbian child and not be terribly uncomfortable with the fact that your child's behavior and lifestyle aren't mainstream. However, you may be having a difficult time dealing with the opinions of others. What others think about you and your child is very important to you, perhaps because you don't have a solid sense of your own self. Then *your beliefs* concerning right and wrong do not matter as much as whether or not *others* view the behavior of your child as "right" or "wrong," "normal" or "abnormal."

You want your child to be accepted by your sister, aunt, or neighbor. You wonder what these people will say when they learn your child is gay, or in some other way falls outside the standards that they view as "normal." Your concern is legitimate. Clearly others *may not* accept your child (and may even blame you) for what your child is or does. But the heart of the matter probably has as much to do with the fear that your sister, aunt, or neighbor will reject you as it does with the fear that they will reject your child.

Focusing on what others will think only reinforces your own insecurity. If you want to get rid of the Velcro of opinion, the real question you will need to consider is, "Why do I let *someone else's opinion* control whether I fully accept my child?"

Temperament

We don't usually pay any more attention to our temperament traits than we do to our choice in sunglasses. Yet different temperament traits are like different colors of sunglasses. Each causes a person to experience the world in a slightly different way, thereby coming to slightly different conclusions concerning what each sees.

The following is a list of temperament traits, each of which will affect the way in which we and our child interact with the world. None of these characteristics is "better" or "worse" than the others. Each person's life contains some of the widely varied threads of human nature: with different temperaments we contribute spice and diversity to the tapestry of life.

Which of these temperament traits apply to you? Which apply to your child?

Quiet and shy or outgoing and quick to speak. Enjoy lots of physical movement and athletic contests or prefer less strenuous activity and a good game of checkers. Active or reserved. Down to earth, factual and practical or able to operate on hunches, imagination, and intuition. Musically talented or tone deaf. Artistically expressive or unable to draw more than stick figures. Compulsive or spontaneous. Able to work on one project at a time before going on to another or able to juggle many different activities. Easily distracted or very focused and concentrated on the task at hand. Decisive and quick or tentative and slow to respond. Emotional or rational. Easy-going or intense. Quick to anger or slow to anger.

Some of these basic personality characteristics can become Velcro for parents who are so used to reacting in one way that they accuse their child of an "unreasonable" stance when all he may be doing is expressing the view of the world as experienced through his temperament.

Temperament differences can also affect the probability, or improbability, that we will become entangled in the lives of our adult children, their spouses, and our grandchildren. For example, if your temperament allows you to be more reserved, if you need lots of time to respond to most situations, it will be easier for you to sit back and reflect on what your adult children say or do. This trait may allow you to see things more objectively. However, if you have always reacted quickly to what goes on around you (as I have a strong inclination to do), it will be more difficult to refrain from getting involved. Your temperament may encourage you to jump to conclusions that are inaccurate because they are based on incomplete information.

So temperament is a factor in how we react to our child. But we must be careful that we do not use temperament characteristics as an "excuse" not to change our behavior, claiming we're just *naturally* quick to speak our mind—and can't do anything about it.

The "Right" Religion

One area of painful conflict between parents and children—that of religion—can produce great quantities of Velcro. Even if we have not practiced our faith for years, we may be extremely disappointed because our daughter has chosen a different religion and is now very active in church activities that exclude us. If we are atheists, we may also be stuck on the issue of religion because our son is a born-again Christian who insists we are damned.

There is something strangely tenacious about the way in which we cling to what we are sure constitutes the most correct theological position, even when we don't believe there is a god. Perhaps this is because we may have convinced ourselves that the greatest test of parenting is the ability to successfully pass on truths we hold so dearly. And if salvation is the main concern of parents, they may be distressed because they fear an errant child will not spend eternity with them. Most disagreements concerning religion, however, tend to focus on behavior, especially when a child denounces her faith or joins one that allows choices that the parents believe are immoral, harmful or irresponsible.

There is no question that all religions encourage certain behaviors and discourage others in order to build community and/or demonstrate allegiance to a deity. These behaviors are generally supposed to be ones of kindness, love, honesty, and hard work. However, during almost sixty years of observing the human condition, I have noticed that behavior often has less to do with outwardly spoken beliefs than with inwardly held beliefs.

There are members of the clergy, to give just one example, who are the kindest people on earth; yet there are also priests and ministers who have sexually molested children. Time and again the world has witnessed members of religions practice aggression, fanaticism, hate, and xenophobia in the name of their faith. Clearly the expression of a faith does not mean a life of service toward all people. I would trust my life with some friends who are faithful believers in an organized religion, with others who are questioning agnostics, and with still others who are atheists strongly opposed to all formal religion. There are also people in those categories I wouldn't trust as far as I could throw them.

If the teachings of religion do not guarantee that a person will respect the rights of others, what does? Why do both religious and non-religious people live lives of deceit or of high ethical standards? I believe the answers are found in the way in which people learn to listen to—or ignore—the wisdom of their own hearts, to that part of us which some call the "soul" and others the "self."

In the center of our being is a quiet voice that says we are all valuable, lovable, and equal. Perhaps the psyche's recognition that every person should be treated humanely merely reflects years of unconsciously absorbing the most kind and nurturing teachings of parents and religion. Yet even people who have been raised by extremely abusive, dishonest, and narcissistic parents know, on a very deep level, that kindness, honesty and generosity are more desirable traits than those they have experienced. In any case, people who pay attention to that intuition generally adhere to the Golden Rule not because they are told they must (although the teachings of their religion may reinforce their behavior), but because to do otherwise would be incongruent with what they feel in their hearts is right.

Many people do not label the inner voice that leads them to choose behaviors that are caring, ethical and responsible as coming from God or even from a benevolent guiding spirit. Some of these people describe themselves as humanists. They view their actions as simply a response to inborn traits that assure the survival of the human race both physically and socially. Others are convinced that the inner voice directing them toward acts of kindness comes from a spiritual source that lies outside the limitations of a person's mind.

This discrepancy in interpretation is not surprising because the *most* important thing that happens when one meditates is the subjective experience itself. The *essence* of how one received a piece of intuition or had a shift in consciousness cannot be captures by description or reduced to a formula.

Nevertheless, an essential element of human nature is the desire to understand what we experience and to share that understanding with others. So the *second* most important thing about such experiences is what we think about them and the *third* most important is how we describe to others the conclusions we have drawn from these elusive experiences. In fact, dogma and creeds have arisen over the centuries in large part because the followers of those religions agree that certain explanations for these "spiritual" experiences make more sense to them than do other interpretations.

It is important to understand that *every* person decides, deep within his heart, which particular ideas and beliefs—out of many points of view available—best explain the mystery of the universe and his place within it.

Like millions of others, you may have unconsciously absorbed your religious philosophy from the culture in which you were raised. In that case your beliefs may feel especially comfortable and have a great deal of support from your community. On the other hand, your views may have grown out of a deliberate and conscious exploration of various doctrines until you finally found one that made the most sense to you. And while your ideas are far different from those of your parents, you may feel as strongly about them as your parents felt about theirs. It is even possible that through your own reflections you have developed a perspective that is unlike that of anyone you know.

If you are stuck in conflict with your child over differences in religious perspectives, you have already discovered that it is almost impossible to win an argument about religion. This is because religion is built not on logic but on beliefs: the belief that there is one god; that the power of the universe is shared by many gods; that there is no divine being; that we only live once; that we return to this world many times; etc. Consequently, at the very least you are unlikely to convince your child by quoting scripture if your child disagrees with the premise on which the holy book is based.

However, you can resolve much of your conflict—without giving up your beliefs—by first answering the following questions as honestly as you are able: "How did I decide which particular explanation of truth was correct, when there are hundreds of interpretations offered by different churches, temples, synagogues and mosques?" "Would I believe what someone told me is true even though it didn't make sense to me?" "Would I consider a person respectful of me if she insisted I accept a belief that did not resonate within the deepest recesses of my heart?" "What prevents me from allowing my child to have her own spiritual experience and from making her own religious decisions?"

After exploring these questions, you may well discover that a discussion of how you came to your conclusions concerning religion and how your child arrived at hers will be enlightening for both of you. You will also discover that some of your Velcro comes off in the process.

The "Right" Race

When our children marry, or marry and divorce and marry again, we are faced with changing family boundaries. When our children decide to add significant others to their lives or one day decide someone is no longer significant, we go through a process of deciding who is family and non-family—who is *in* and who will be left *out*. These decisions can uncover much Velcro we hadn't noticed before.

Since some people are naturally "inclusive," they may comfortably consider in-laws, ex-in-laws, the relatives of in-laws, and good friends as "family." However, such extended families are not as comfortable for those who tend to be more "exclusive," who define families in much more limited terms. And when adult children date or marry people who do not fit the stereotype of what they consider their "in" group, all hell can break loose. This is *especially* true when the family is asked to expand its membership to include an individual from another race or ethnic group.

Parents confronted with in-laws of a different race or culture react in many different ways. The most extreme, of course, are fanatics who can see almost no good in another racial group. Wanting clear separation of the races, they may disown their children or, at the very least, refuse to have anything to do with their son- or daughter-in-law or grandchildren. However, the majority of parents are probably more like Maria, the woman I discussed in the second chapter. They aren't without some degree of prejudice, but they are mostly concerned for what the future will hold for their child's mixed marriage in a society filled with prejudice and ethnic conflict.

Clearly race is a Velcro issue for many parents. We cannot easily dismiss our stereotypes. However, for those of us stuck uncomfortably in conflicts or disappointment over race and nationality, the question we might consider is how much we unconsciously project our own sense of inadequacies onto others.

An editorial in TIME addresses this aspect of race. Lance Morrow, following the Clarence Thomas-Anita Hill senate hearings, wrote,

> *The Thomas proceedings had an unexpected cleansing power where race is concerned. The antagonists were black. The drama was universal. The crime of racism is to deny the humanity of people with skin of a different color. Tolerance arises from a recognition of oneself in others, from seeing in a separate being all one's own possibilities, weakness, appetites, loves, lapses, brutalities, decencies. The leading players in the Thomas drama, and many in the supporting cast, were accomplished, gifted, attractive, ambitious, complicated Americans— and in this case, incidentally, African Americans. The hearings called forth a procession of people diverse and successful in ways not normally visible to white America.*

The question we must each consider is whether we accept in ourselves our own "possibilities, weakness, appetites, loves, lapses, brutalities, decencies." When we are able to do that, we will no longer need to project those qualities onto others. Then which race is "best" or "right" will no longer be an important issue.

Our Success Reflected in Our Child's Achievements

The success or failure of our children in the arena of work is a Velcro issue for many parents. This Velcro is more than the typical assumption by most parents that their children will do at least as well as they have done, or better. It arises when we are disappointed that our children don't seem to be ambitious enough to achieve what we think they can achieve. We can commiserate with a recession layoff and with disruption in the job market when plants close. And if our child is *unable* to handle more than he does, we know he is doing as well as he can. However, when our child is *capable*, but lacks the ambition to be "successful," doesn't even *want* to get there, we can be very disappointed.

And what is this success for which we want our child to strive? For many it is not unlike the King of the Mountain game we enjoyed as children. Getting to the top. Being the best. But notice that the winner is on top only because he has been tougher and more capable of outwitting opponents. He will stay there only until someone stronger and smarter comes along. Being on top is like building houses on the sand. Permanence is impossible. The one who makes it to the top must keep scrambling to stay there, never quite able to relax and enjoy the prize, always needing to look over his shoulders to see who is catching up.

Not all parents view success in this way, of course. Some did the best they could in their job, and if things gradually evolved so that they ended up at the top, all the better; but they would have been satisfied with less. They don't ask more of their children. Many other parents have been quite happy in jobs that asked far less of them than they were capable of doing. After graduation from high school or college they may have taken a job that did not challenge them, but because they enjoyed what they did and didn't feel a need to scramble for a higher position, they have been satisfied with their careers. When their child also seems to follow a less challenging path than he is capable of handling, they tend to accept the situation fairly easily.

How we parents react to our child's level of "success" or "failure" in the world of work will depend in large part on how we ourselves define success and on whether we see ourselves as having met those standards.

If we believe we have "failed," the reason for our failure can keep us focused on our child's success, or lack of it. Did we fail despite conscientious effort and determination because our job required more technical training than we had received? Or did we not make the grade because we didn't put in the effort, and are still kicking ourselves for our lack of ambition? Until we come to terms with what it means that we have failed, or succeeded, we are unlikely to let our child succeed or fail in his own right. *When our child's success needs to be a vicarious victory for us, we deny our child the right to succeed on his own terms.*

Family Patterns that Prevent Conflict Resolution

Our communication and conflict resolution skills have much to do with our ability, or inability, to resolve issues between us and our children. In many ways these patterns, often handed down from parent to child in that multi-generational transmission process I talked about in the third chapter, can be thought of as another form of Velcro.

If you and your child have been taking turns jerking that rope back and forth across your differences of opinion; or if you pretend you've dropped the rope but keep it close at hand; or if the rope has gotten so entangled you don't know where it begins or ends, the examples below may provide a context in which you can understand how you learned ineffective approaches to conflict.

Emotional and Physical Cutoff

Have you and your child not spoken for years? If so, then there is a good chance that members in your family resolved conflict by simply cutting themselves off, emotionally or physically, from those with whom they disagreed. This is a version of the childhood game of see-things-my-way-or-I'll-take-my-marbles-and-leave. This method of resolving conflict doesn't *resolve* the conflict, of course. The participants simply *act* as though there is no problem, or as though they aren't bothered by the disagreement that caused the cutoff. Certainly cutting off a family member is a powerful anesthetic that can reduce emotional pain. It can also leave a huge hole in the fabric of the family.

If this is your style, you might want to ask yourself what you gain by refusing to communicate with your child. Do you get to feel righteous as long as your child is viewed as stubborn and wrong? Or has your child cut you off because you have insisted she view her childhood as you see it, not as she sees it? Have you set it up so the only way your child can return into the family graces is to agree with you and so lose face?

On the other hand, you may not be in contact with your child despite your best ability to work through your differences. Further contact at this juncture may be pointless and only embroil all of you in unending turmoil. If you have given your child every opportunity to work things out amiably, then your cutoff may not be a Velcro issue. However, you will still need to deal with your grief, if you have not already done so, and to bring closure to your relationship as you move on with your life.

Physical or Emotional Illness

Does your family always have someone "sick" who needs to be cared for? And does that person often manage to get ill at those times when he could get maximum attention? Is there an alcoholic or drug abuser on whom the family has focused much of its energy?

The struggles necessary to resolve differences of opinion are avoided in some families by shifting focus from the *conflict* that needs attention to a *person* who needs attention, poor thing. For example, the mother of a client of mine always got a headache when my client wanted to talk about serious family matters. The pain of the headache may have been real. The inability of the family to resolve their issues was also real.

If this is the kind of problem-avoidance that was used in your family, perhaps you have unintentionally passed this trait on to your son. Perhaps he gets sick and becomes unable to function whenever you start to insist he has to get a job or find his own apartment. Or perhaps you feel tightness in your chest when your daughter wants to go on vacation and asks you to baby-sit. While you love your grandchildren, their bad manners get on your nerves. Your pain may be the only method you know that allows you to get out of unpleasant chores. You haven't yet learned how to say simply, "Sorry, Sue, I don't want the responsibility of caring for your five children for a week."

Manipulation

It is very hard to resolve conflicts with our child if we are unwilling to directly address the issues that divide us. And in some families being *indirect* is a way of life. If you were raised in a family in which confrontation was anathema and indirect manipulation was the modus operandi, you may find it terribly difficult, if not impossible, to make any real progress in getting past disagreements with your child.

It was many years before I realized that my mother frequently got what she wanted from my father by using a maneuver I call going-all-around-the-barn-to-get-in-the-barn-door, a technique I also used before I discovered it is much easier to head straight for the door. And a friend of mine said that in her home you couldn't ask directly for another piece of bread. You had to ask others at the table if *they* would like to have one and then, as the plate was being passed around, you could take a slice.

Edith, the mother of Jill, a client of mine, is a master of the art of manipulation. When driving in the car she will ask others if they are cold. If they then ask her directly if *she* wants the heater turned on, she will respond, "If you do, dear." When the family discusses which restaurant they want to go to, Edith will say, "I don't care. You all choose." Later, she will wonder with a sigh of disappointment why the others didn't select such-and-such a place.

Individuals who are afraid of face-to-face conflict may hide behind a facade of sweet innocence, but they are masters at getting others to give them what they want. They are also masters at playing "yes-but" with every potential solution that is offered directly. And, like Edith, they expect others to read their minds.

There is no doubt that having others read our minds protects us from the discomfort of having our requests rejected openly if we were to state our views outright. On the other hand, mind reading is a terribly inefficient system for getting our needs met and contributes to half-hearted discussions that lead nowhere. It can also give rise to a lot of resentment when others fail to interpret our needs correctly.

Unsatisfying Relationships

A Velcro issue for some parents can be observed when they pay undue attention to an adult child's problems as an avoidance of dealing with marital issues or as a handy distraction from the loneliness of being single. If you are a parent who looks for problems in your child's life because you don't know how to straighten out problems in your love life, this is the time to do something about it.

Until now you may have avoided taking action because you fear an honest appraisal will mean either that you and your partner will have to split up (which seems a horrendous prospect) or that you must stick together in misery (which may seem equally horrendous). But your catastrophic ruminations are, most likely, fears that will not materialize. A careful analysis of your situation—and even a decision to stop living a life of dissatisfaction—will almost certainly lead to a conclusion far less disastrous than you expect. You may well be better off and happier apart!

Studies of life after divorce do not paint nearly as pessimistic a scene as our myths would have us believe. After an initial period of adjustment, even older women are discovering their lives are much fuller and more satisfying when they are no longer in deadening marriages. Those who were previously defined by how well their husbands succeeded discover who they are in their own right. In small incremental steps they can rekindle desires and occupations put away with their wedding dress. With new freedom comes a different, exciting view of the world. New and expanded friendships provide a wonderful base of support. Consequently, while deciding to leave a miserable marriage is not, obviously, a piece of cake, it is frequently a tremendous change for the better. Life does not need to be spent in a miserable marriage until the bitter end.

On the other hand, it is never too late to learn how to communicate effectively with your spouse and to enjoy your remaining years together.

Start by making a thorough list of what you like and don't like about your relationship. An objective appraisal of your life together may very likely uncover more pluses than minuses. You may be surprised to discover that "desirable" and "undesirable" traits (both yours and your partner's) have complemented each other nicely over the years. As one woman told me, "I may not have a perfect marriage and often don't feel close to my husband. But I have decided to be satisfied with what I have. I don't confront him because it has never worked to do that. We agree on religious issues that are important to us both and he still goes out with me on Friday night dates, as we've been doing for twenty years, so it's not as though everything is wrong."

Her statement illustrates how we all make compromises. Not many of us can have *everything* the way we want, or even the way we deserve. Some people, like this woman, consciously choose not to confront their partners about what bothers them.

And if *not* having a partner has caused you to focus on your child, this is a good time to expand your social network. Friends of both sexes can offer distraction from expending energy on noticing how well, or poorly, your child is doing.

So if you suspect that your focus on issues in your child's life derives some of its energy from your avoidance of marital or couples issues, you can kill two birds with one stone, so to speak. When you work on whatever it is that bugs you about your partner, you will not be as bugged by what your child does.

We Sacrificed for Our Child and Now We Don't Get No Respect

When we consider the amount of time, money, and effort we have put into child rearing, it is not surprising we sometimes feel let down when a child doesn't turn out as expected. We may wonder what practical use our child will ever make of the opportunities we gave him (opportunities many of us did not have as children). Nevertheless, most of us don't expect our child to "pay us back."

But too often children become, as Elinor Lenz says, "instrumentalities of parental sacrifice—that is, the parents, in making certain 'sacrifices' on behalf of the children, are seeking to fulfill themselves through the children. To construe parental self-denial as a promissory note that must be repaid on demand is like saddling someone with a debt that he or she was unaware of taking on."

This Velcro issue might be called "the Rodney Dangerfield complaint." The parents focus on the fact that their children don't give them the respect they believe they deserve.

Rachel and Harry, whose story I heard several years ago, illustrate what happens when parents fail to recognize that *their* goals do not automatically translate into the goals of their children.

> *Rachel and Harry had denied themselves many things so that Julie could take dancing lessons, and they were extremely proud that Julie was a prize pupil. She was about to apply for a dance scholarship when she met John, who swept her off her dancing feet and into a quick marriage. Her parents were angry and told her so, in no uncertain terms.*
>
> *Julie's response? She stopped visiting them. Eventually the relationship became so strained that she refused even to talk to them any more. Rachel and Harry feel terribly rejected both by her decision to discontinue dance and her alienation from them. They fail to understand that their inability to let go of their ambition for her became their Velcro and got in the way of what could have been a satisfying relationship.*

Is What They Say True, or Isn't It?

Today many parents are confronted by adult children who insist their parents were dysfunctional or that one or both were alcoholic. Other children claim they have recently uncovered memories of being sexually molested by a neighbor, grandfather, uncle or, even worse, their parent. Such accusations have increasingly created a wedge between parents and their children.

In other cases parents are forced to look at behavior of their child that has serious physical or legal consequences. For example, their friends try to tell them that the brilliant mind of their talented child has been damaged by drugs. The police insist their son is not innocent, as he claims, of charges that he exposed himself in public, or had sex with a minor, or swindled his girlfriend.

If you have had to face these kinds of accusations, what have you said? Your response would seem a fairly simple matter because, after all, if you have been accused of something, you either did it or you didn't. If you did it, you either remember doing it or you don't. If you remember, you either admit it or you don't. Yet if you are like most people, you will, at first, deny such accusations—whether or not they are true.

Denial Serves a Purpose

If you are heavily invested in *protecting your child's reputation*, you will deny what others say about him. Unless you see your son shove cocaine up his nose, you will refuse to believe—or at least to acknowledge to others—that he is not the innocent child you once held on your knee. After all, to admit your child would do such terrible things is paramount to admitting that you didn't raise him right; to openly condemn him may seem to be the same as condemning yourself.

If you are heavily invested in *protecting your reputation*, you will adamantly deny any accusation others make against you. Unless they hold incontrovertible evidence, you will insist they cannot possibly be right. If the accusation is sexual abuse, you may go through several stages of denial—even if you eventually acknowledge you were fully responsible. You may at first deny the facts, claiming the abuse never happened. When you continue to be challenged, however, and if more than one person comes forward to accuse you, this denial may fall away and you may go through several other forms of denial. Denial you knew what you were doing. Denial of responsibility. Denial of the impact your action had on the person you abused.

Denial is especially understandable in cases of incest, for as a *Family Therapy Networker* article points out:

> *Denial is a universal human defense against bad news, and almost no news is worse for a family and the individuals in it than the discovery of incest. Of all the problems that can haunt families—alcohol abuse, infidelity, violence, abandonment—nothing evokes as much shame, guilt and fear in family members, and as much disgust, rage and incomprehension in outsiders, as incest. Faced with making a disclosure that threatens to shred every vestige of familial love, security and respect, incestuous families live with cognitive dissonance that almost forces them to deny the abuse.*

Even if the accusation is far less serious than sexual abuse, it is not surprising that we deny, at least initially, accusations against us or our child. As Carol Pearson points out, "We give things up little by little. That's the psychological reason for denial—it keeps us from having to confront all our problems at once!" Denial is a protective device that can give you time to take a deep breath before you sort through whatever it is you have been accused of denying.

While incest is viewed as the worst-case scenario, it is also extremely difficult for parents to admit they were guilty of physical or emotional abuse, neglect or abandonment, alcoholism, or chemical dependency. And it often isn't much easier to deal with accusations of parenting mistakes that are of a far less serious nature. It is especially difficult to struggle through such a confrontation if we believe the accusation has absolutely no basis in fact.

And as difficult as an accusation can be for the parent who is accused of a serious offense, the other parent must also deal with ramifications of the accusation. Almost always the question is raised as to why the other parent didn't protect the child. Did the mother know what her husband did in the middle of the night, but feel powerless to stop it? Did the father suspect that his wife was beating the children when he was at work, but do nothing to interfere?

How Can You Respond to an Accusation by Your Child?

If your child has falsely accused either you or your spouse of abuse of any kind or has strongly criticized some parenting decisions you feel were wise, you have my deepest sympathy. It takes a great deal of courage to maintain balance in the middle of an extremely unsettling situation like this one. And the circumstances aren't much better if you agree that some of what you are accused of doing was not right, or in the best interest of the child, but still believe your behavior was not sufficiently serious to warrant such accusation.

Nevertheless, if you want to have a genuine connection with your child *and* she has made an accusation that you did, or continue to, engage in some activity that caused her harm, you can only get past the stalemate of accusations and denials by facing the issues directly.

The process of healing will require you to keep two attitudes firmly in mind.

First, you must realize that no matter how clear your memory may seem to you, you do not recall the past accurately. Memory is a creative process in which events are overlaid with interpretations taught by successive experience. A memory at age twenty-five may be quite different from a memory about that same event when we are fifty-five. To put it another way, *your memory* of your daughter's childhood is not the way it happened any more than *her memory* of what happened is exactly what happened. You will both have memories of what occurred and they both contain kernels of truth.

The second attitude needed for a resolution of your problem is respect for the person who is asking you to see her life, and you, in a different light. *Respect means you will need to listen to one another and be open to the possibility that there may have been some negative effect you had on the other person, even though you did not intend to harm that person.*

Is Your Child Telling the Truth About Sexual Abuse?

Since there are seldom witnesses to incest, how can the truth be known if the incident supposedly happened many years ago? This question is at the center of every accusation of abuse based on memories retrieved in adulthood.

Recently the term "false memory syndrome" was coined to describe cases in which a person believes she has been sexually abused when in fact nothing of the sort has happened. In recent years there have been several cases in which families have been torn apart and good reputations have been ruined through such false allegations.

Criticism of therapists in these cases is understandable, especially if the supposed memories have been created by hypnosis and result from the relentless implication of abuse where there was none. There are probably therapists who have not resolved their own rage about the abuse they suffered and who use clients, perhaps unconsciously, as proxies in an effort to seek justice. Sometimes clients have read so much material on the wounded inner child that they have convinced themselves that they are incest survivors without having recovered any memories at all.

Having said all this, I must also state that *most* accusations of abuse are considered by reputable therapists to be legitimate. I know from my own experience as a therapist that when memories of abuse surface, the process gradually unfolds with great reluctance, sleep disturbances, thoughts of suicide, and profound feelings of shame. Clients *fight* the memories that intrude into their lives, offering them an unwanted view of their childhood. It is extremely difficult to believe anyone would deliberately put herself through this hell because she psychologically needed a catharsis for some strange reason. The payoff is great pain and, often, estrangement from her family.

Is it Possible You Just Don't Remember What You Did?

Since this book is written from the perspective of the parent accused of abuse, what is the possibility that you did, in fact, abuse your child and simply don't remember doing so?

There are many men who, in a state of drunkenness, may fondle their stepdaughter's breast and later be unable to remember what they have done. There are parents who suffered sexual abuse at the hands of *their* parents or guardians and who have repressed their memories of it. When they then have children, they may, for example, wash their child's genitals longer and more roughly than necessary in an *unconscious* reaction to abuse they have not yet dealt with. Many years later, when that child (the grandchild of the person who began the cycle of abuse) becomes an adult, she may recall those baths with a realization that as a child she sensed that her boundaries were somehow invaded. But back then she could not object or put words to her feelings. Now she may accuse her unsuspecting parent of having sexually abused her. The parent will, of course, deny there were any sexual overtones in those baths so long ago—if she has not yet dealt with her own abuse.

However, most sexual abuse is not forgotten or repressed by the perpetrator. It is only denied. Parents who abused their child over a period of many weeks, months and years know what they have done. They simply deny because they want to protect themselves from the consequences that any exposure of their acts will bring upon them and their families.

I do not believe that if someone adamantly denies an accusation that his very denial is in any way evidence of his guilt. (There are those who feel that the more someone denies an accusation, the more likely it is true.) And I certainly don't intend to offer judgment on whether or not you are guilty of things your child accuses you of.

However, if you've been less than honest in your response to an accusation—and you know whether or not you have been—you are in an extremely difficult position. It is terribly hard to keep secret the knowledge that you have done something society considers taboo—and hoping desperately that no one will bring it to light. That secret must surely create a hell all its own. Yet one of the most cleansing experiences of life occurs when we unburden ourselves of what we have been trying for years to hide. That has always been the power of confession. And if you are carrying such a burden, this *could* be the time to unload it so that you can find peace at last.

"I'm Sorry, But . . . . ."

On the surface of it, it would seem that the matter of apologies to our children, whether for acts of serious abuse or minor errors resulting from uneven parenting, is rather straightforward. We recognize that we weren't perfect parents when our child was young and may still make mistakes. We tell that to our child. Our child is glad to hear our apology, to have his needs acknowledged openly. End of story.

Unfortunately, it's not so easy, in many cases.

Let me give you an example. My client Jill, whom I mentioned earlier in this chapter when I spoke of manipulation and mind reading, finally decided to confront her mother, Edith, with the fact that she would never come out and ask for what she wanted directly. Jill also wanted Edith to accept her just as she was and to pay attention to her; for her mother could turn almost any subject Jill initiated into a discussion of her own life or what was happening to her mother's friends. Jill's mother isn't any different today from the way she was when Jill was young. Edith has always been reluctant to state her needs directly and Jill has always been the dutiful daughter who had to figure out her mother's emotional needs and take care of them.

Edith's approach to life seems to stem from the fact that she and her infant sister were given up for adoption when she was three. The other five children in the family remained with their father, who felt he could not cope with seven children after his wife died. The conclusion young Edith drew was that she would still be with her parents if she had only been a better girl. Best not to rock the boat and openly demand too much or what you have will be taken from you.

What does Edith's childhood have to do with apologies? To begin with, she learned very early to use manipulation to get her needs met because asking directly was forbidden. And because she decided she had to always be "good," she later developed the persona of a perfect mother, fearing abandonment if anyone caught her making a mistake. There is no doubt that *she tried very hard to be a good mother*. But she was imperfect, of course, as all mothers are in one way or another; she *did* fail her daughter in several ways.

When Edith was confronted by Jill, it took a long time for her to acknowledge any mistakes. After all, she'd tried so hard! And so when she finally apologized, it went something like this. "I'm sorry, Jill, but you know I've always tried to do my best and it's been hard for me because your father wasn't always there when I needed him and I suppose that I've always tried so hard because I was adopted as a little girl and thought I could bring back my parents if I would only do things right and so I . . . ."

A simple, "I'm sorry," or "I'm sorry I wasn't there for you," or "I'm sorry I turn your stories into an opportunity to talk about myself" would have sufficed. When our children were young, we *all* failed to be there for them one hundred percent of the time. The reasons are irrelevant.

Perhaps you see yourself as a terrible failure because you were an alcoholic when your child was young. You broke many promises to your child and failed to attend back-to-school night because you were drinking with friends. Now you've joined AA and consider your drinking to be a disease. You offer that explanation for your behavior when you apologize to your child. But your child did not experience a disease. Your child experienced a mother or father who broke promises and didn't attend school events like the other kids' parents.

The reason *why* we were imperfect parents is not nearly as important as the fact that we were. There may come a time when we may want to discuss with our child how we came to be the parents we were. We may want to talk about our shame of being an alcoholic or drug abuser or how our own parents abused us or failed us. Insights into our parent behavior are not unimportant. For starters, however, a simple apology is the best way to remove the Velcro of guilt.

One more word about apologies before we leave the subject.

We are all entitled to feel the way we feel. In fact, "entitled" isn't even an appropriate word when it comes to emotions. There is no granting of rights or entitlements that *allow* us to feel what we feel. Yet often parents get caught in the *Velcro of non-apology* because, while they can acknowledge they weren't perfect parents, they feel their child has gone overboard in her reaction to how her parents guided her through The Parenting Game.

If your daughter says she was extremely angry you didn't let her take horseback riding lessons, even though you could afford them, do you find yourself resisting an apology because you think her reaction is inappropriate? After all, you did what you thought was best in having her take piano lessons instead. But what difference does it make if you thought you were giving her the "better" kind of lessons? You missed understanding her deep desire to ride a horse. A simple statement, "I'm sorry I didn't realize you wanted riding lessons so badly" is enough. And again, no explanations are necessary.

I'll Change if You Change

One of the stickiest pieces of Velcro has to do with the popular game of you-go-first—offering to make adjustments in our behavior once the other person has stopped doing the things that drive us crazy.

What if that never happens? After all, there ain't no guarantee that our child is ever going to do what we want him to do! If we get our energy to pull on the rope from the hope that our efforts will pay off, our energy supply is likely to diminish year by year if our child remains as stubborn as we are. Before long we will be left with nothing but sore muscles to show for our efforts.

Instead, I'd like to suggest a miracle. That's right. A miracle. It goes something like this.

Suppose, just suppose, that during the night a miracle has happened and the problem between you and your child is resolved. There is no longer any conflict and dissension. You have both stopped pulling on the rope! However, since you were sleeping when this happened, you didn't know about it. But when other people see you, *they* can tell something about you is different, something that could only be possible if the problem with your child no longer consumed so much of your energy.

So what is it that would be different about you if a miracle happened? Would there be a lightness in your step if you stopped pulling on the rope? Would you look more peaceful and be more patient with others? Would the worry lines leave your face? Would you speak more kindly about your child?

And how about your interests in life? What would you do with your time if you were no longer occupied in staring at your child across the rift that previously separated you? What would you do with your money now that you no longer needed to rescue a thirty-five-year-old daughter who was unable to resist buying things on impulse and frequently needed a loan she never repaid? What kind of life would you make for yourself if you and your child accepted each other's right to have different values, to make choices, to make mistakes?

There's no doubt about it. If your problem *were* resolved, if there were no rift between you and your child, your behavior and attitude toward life would be different. There is also no doubt about the fact that you can change your behavior and attitude toward life even if the differences between you and your child *remain* unresolved to your satisfaction.

You might try waking up tomorrow and assuming a miracle has happened. After all, all you have to lose are the worry lines on your face and the tension in your body.

Qualities Both We and Our Children Need

As we near the end of this discussion of Velcro issues, I want to point out an antidote to the development of Velcro—spiritual qualities essential for healthy living. Just as the fabric of our lives is woven in part from our temperament, the fabric also reflects the ways in which we express such qualities as integrity, courage, beauty, kindness, generosity, creativity, forgiveness, love, honesty, joy, patience, serenity.

It is true that some of these qualities are perhaps more easily achieved by those with one temperament than another and by those who are raised in families in which they were encouraged. Nevertheless, they are all available to all of us if we open ourselves to them. And the more of them we express the more we will experience the world, including ourselves and our child, from a more compassionate perspective.

Consider the case of Harriet and her son Paul on page 79-80. As you may recall, Harriet was disturbed because Paul lacked self-motivation and determination, traits she herself was missing. However, we could look at her story in a slightly different light; as one in which the problem stemmed from her lack of the quality of acceptance. She was not able to accept her son just as he was. Whether or not he accepted her was not the issue.

Not only do spiritual qualities make letting go easier, they can soften the conflicts that naturally happen when people with different lives and different points of view are related. For example, if we are flexible we don't become inordinately upset if our daughter has to change her plans and can't go on vacation with us. If there is joy in our lives, we are less likely to get bent out of shape if our child goes a bit overboard and enjoys playing more than studying or climbing the ladder of success. And like Kipling's Kim, if we can remain calm in the face of chaos, the upheavals in our child's life will not turn us upside down.

Removing Our Velcro

We can get out of the Velcro Syndrome as soon as we recognize that our opinions and behaviors (our piece of Velcro) get caught by our child's opinions and behavior (his piece of Velcro) AND we decide to do something about it. Identifying the problem is half the battle.

No matter what our particular Velcro issue has been, we can learn to accept our child without giving up our own values and beliefs. We can learn to stop insisting that our rules for behavior be followed, to relax some of the high standards we hold for ourselves and others, to be less concerned about what others think. We can learn to allow our child to define success on his terms and not ours, or to stop rescuing our child from the financial difficulties into which he often slides. We can learn to listen to what our child is trying to say without shutting her out just because her opinions seem bizarre and foreign, to stop using our child as a shield that hides our own needs. And finally, we can stop feeling guilty.

To approach life in a new way, to think, see and act differently, requires us to learn what we didn't know before. Fortunately, there is a phrase that can help us make that transition, especially if we have a tendency to kick ourselves for not having the hindsight we could have used long ago. The phrase is simply, "Up until now I haven't known how to . . . ."

This statement is very powerful in supporting change because it implies that, while it is true you may not have known something in the past, today you can tell yourself that, "Until now I haven't known how to end pointless arguments with my daughter." With this statement you affirm the real possibility that you *can* learn to stop tugging on the rope in a futile effort to get your child to see your point of view.

And when you have changed, you will discover that one of the best things about removing Velcro is the benefit you will experience in many parts of your life. If nothing else, you will expend a lot less energy defending your position, energy you can put to better use. And when you realize that there are many interpretations of truth, you may discover, as other parents have, that it is fun to have conversations with your adult children. You may even learn something from them in the process.

The best way I can end this chapter is to give you a poem by Portia Nelson that appears in Claudia Black's book, *Repeat After Me*. It describes what happens when we finally discover the way in which we are stuck and no longer need to be stuck, or, in the metaphor of the poem, when we no longer fall blindly into a hole.

An Autobiography in Five Short Chapters

I

I walk down the street.
There is a deep hole in the sidewalk.
I fall in
I am lost . . . I am helpless.
It isn't my fault.
It takes forever to find a way out.

II

I walk down the same street.
There is a deep hole in the sidewalk.
I pretend I don't see it.
I fall in again.
I can't believe I am in the same place.
But it isn't my fault.
It still takes a long time to get out.

III

I walk down the same street.
There is a deep hole in the sidewalk.
I see it is there.
I still fall in . . .it's a habit.
My eyes are open.
I know where I am.
It is my fault.
I get out immediately.

IV

I walk down the same street.
There is a deep hole in the sidewalk.
I walk around it.

V

I walk down another street.

Chapter 7

The Heart Slowly Heals

At this stage in our healing journey we enter a period of transformation. When we release lost dreams and forgive ourselves and others, we begin to see the light at the end of the tunnel, even though it may still be dark where we stand.

Perhaps you have worked on some of your Velcro issues and have recognized that your firmly held convictions have denied your child the right to his own. Even after you have done all this, however, you may discover that you are not yet ready to let go completely with love. Your unreleased expectations, unmourned dreams, old resentments and guilt may stand in your way. Therefore, grieving and forgiveness are your major tasks in this fourth stage of healing.

Since work on these issues is usually easier to address after you've at least partly untangled yourself from your child's problems, this chapter follows the one on the Velcro Syndrome. However, it is not unusual for parents to move back and forth between the third and fourth stages as they make their way along this road of healing.

The Need to Release Lost Dreams

Your child does not need to die or refuse to see you in order for you to experience a deep sense of loss. Your child does not need to live on the streets, as my son did for several years, for you to have almost constant pain. Much less serious situations are also experiences as painful, even though you may not feel "entitled" to express that pain because it seems so "trivial."

You want to support your child's decision not to enter the family business and may tell him it's okay with you. But it really isn't. You want to be accepting of your son when he tells you he is gay; you don't remind him of your hopes for grandchildren. However, you envy your friend's new grandchild and are sad that you will probably never know what a grandchild of yours will look like.

When our child has failed to meet our expectations and dreams, both large and small, where do those dreams go?

For some parents, unfulfilled expectations are not much of an issue. They would have *preferred* that things turned out differently, of course, but they approach life in a manner that allows them to readjust their dreams readily when circumstances change.

Other parents revel in the past. Every day they open their drawer of memories and examine all the things that have been and all the dreams they had. If some of those dreams were not fulfilled, they can't possibly let go of them. Releasing dreams means they may have to find new ones to take their place. Dreams require looking forward, and they haven't learned to look through that window.

Probably the majority of disappointed parents take a middle road between these two extremes when they realize their child is marching to a different drum beat than the one they played for him as a child. Most of the time they don't obsess over what has happened. Nevertheless, the expectations and dreams they had for their child return quietly in the night, unbidden, but reminding them that they are still around and unattended.

"Attending to" lost dreams, so that their pain is relieved and finally healed, is what grief work for disappointed parents is all about.

Many parents, unfortunately, feel it would be self-pity if they thought about their lost dreams. But it is not *self-pity* to grieve for what you wanted and don't have. Rather, it is *self-care* when you grieve the loss of what you hoped for your family—*so that those dreams can rest in peace and you can move on to letting go with love for your child and peace in your heart.*

Consider the stories of two parents who don't realize that releasing past expectations and dreams can lift a weight from their hearts. Could you identify with their pain?

The first example, the mother of a son sentenced to life in prison, feels locked with him in "a nightmare that never ends." If this were you, would you also avoid old friends who may not know what your son has done, so that you won't have to tell them? Would you also avoid meeting new people because, when others get to talking about their families, which they eventually will, you can't bring yourself to tell anyone about your son's situation? Please believe me when I say that such a nightmare does not need to dominate your life, even though your pain will never completely go away.

The other example is the father who is greatly disappointed because his son didn't choose the prestigious college he had long planned for him to attend (or maybe his son couldn't get in, or flunked out). If the expectation you had for your child is similar to this, you will probably discover that there is a tug in your heart every time you talk with your friends about their "successful" sons (or are otherwise reminded of an expectation that wasn't met)—until you deal with the grief of having a son who did not receive the education you think he *should have* received.

Learning to Grieve

Grieving is intended to accomplish two major and intertwining psychological tasks. The first is to acknowledge and accept the truth—that what you wanted you do not have. The second is to experience and deal with all the emotions that the loss of your expectations create for you as a parent.

To work through and complete the grief involved in releasing your dreams you will need to accept your feelings openly and honestly for however long it takes for the wound to heal. That doesn't mean you have to wear your heartache on your sleeve. But you must be willing, at least within the privacy of your heart, to admit that you are grieving. For most of us, that is a big order.

It takes courage to grieve. However, if we *don't* have the courage to grieve, we draw the drapes across our windows and then complain because the sun doesn't shine into our house.

Grief Requires a New Self-identity

Part of your self-identity at one time may have been as "the parent of a son who was going to make something of himself." Now, however, when your son has no job and doesn't seem inclined to want one or keep it for long, your self-identity needs readjustment. You may resist giving up your old identity if you believe you must now see yourself as "a parent who failed to teach my son to be responsible." Fortunately, there are alternatives.

In forging a new identity, the challenge is to *reframe the undesired definition into one that does not connect your identity with that of your child.* For example, you can decide to say, "I am the parent of a son who has chosen a lifestyle that is very different from mine. He is a separate person and *I am not defined by what he does, but by who I am.*" This is the statement I learned when I needed to change my identity to reflect the reality in my family.

Another example: You considered yourself to be "a parent who used firm but kind discipline." Now your child claims she was emotionally abused by you and has been in therapy "to heal her wounded child." Even though you acknowledge that your high standards may have sometimes been too strict and you did not always take her needs into account, you can't quite see yourself as "a parent who abused my child." A reframing for you could be, "I am a parent who tried my best to discipline my child, and while agreeing I may have made some mistakes, I release my daughter to view her childhood in the way she chooses. I am sorry for the pain I unintentionally caused her."

Clear Boundaries Allow Us to Grieve in Our Own Way

One of the difficulties in letting go of lost dreams (and also in dealing with guilt) is the fact that we often need others to support us through the process by understanding what we are going through. Consequently, we can become distressed when our spouse or partner does not view the situation the same way we do. That was certainly my problem. It took me a very long time to accept the fact that just because Bob and I did not respond to our disappointment in the same way did not mean that he wasn't disappointed, or that he wasn't grieving in his own, more private, way.

If your spouse clearly accepts your child's choices and lifestyle while you definitely do not, you will experience the pain of broken dreams and he or she will not. Or your partner may need to talk and talk and talk, while you need silence for your grief to work itself out.

These differences can interfere with the grieving process if you have allowed your boundaries to mesh with those of your spouse; that is, if you assume you both have the same needs and characteristics. Such unclear boundaries do not just create problems for the grieving process. They can also interfere with your ability to let go of your adult child. After all, how can you let go of another person if you can't tell where he ends and you begin? Letting go of him can feel like cutting off a piece of yourself.

Here is a simple exercise that can help create boundaries between you and others. It's good for you and your partner, you and your child, you and anyone else you have a hard time seeing as a clearly separate individual.

Imagine you have rolled some gingerbread dough onto a cookie sheet, taken two different cookie cutters, with different features, and pressed them into the dough to form two separate gingerbread people. If the dough is baked without any further attention, the cookies will come out of the oven all in one piece. There must be *space* between the cookies in order for the cookie people to be separate and distinct from one another. Therefore, before you put the cookies in the oven, you must take a knife and cut away the dough that lies between the gingerbread people so that both cookies can bake and expand separately, with distinct characteristics and boundaries.

Like cookies, we need space between us to define who we are. When you find yourself becoming upset that someone is not seeing things the way you do, notice whether you have allowed your boundaries to intermingle with another person. Imagine that you can use a magic sword to create a clear boundary around who you are and who the other person is. Imagine that now, instead of being held together like two fused cookies, you are gently and softly connected with love. This not only will reinforce your sense of self, it will help you respect the other person as having a right to be different.

Working Through the Emotions of Grief

There are many emotions involved as disappointed parents move through the grief process. The intensity of those feelings, as well as the way in which we express them, varies from parent to parent. Yet few are immune to the powerful emotions that lost dreams can generate, especially feelings of sadness and depression.

When we can't imagine an end to deep family rifts, our situation can appear as a bottomless chasm into which we've fallen. To seek relief from the torment of deep pain and depression, some parents may wish their child would simply disappear, may regret the child was born or may even wish they, or their child, would die! It has been interesting to see the reaction of people who trusted me enough, because of the grief I've been through in my own situation, to tell me they felt this way at times. They were extremely relieved to discover that I understood, for they felt terrible in thinking such thoughts. Most said they had never told anyone else that sometimes these "solutions" had seemed the only way they could ever get out of the deep hole in which they found themselves.

However, once parents accept the challenge to focus on themselves rather than on their child, their deep depression almost always begins to lift. They begin to look around and see they might escape from their hole.

There are many ways in which you can gradually lessen the hold of depression. One of my favorites is through the use of family pictures, allowing your sadness to surface so that it can then be washed away.

Look at several pictures of your child when he was young. What were your dreams for him? What dreams did he have for himself? Allow yourself to feel the pain of the loss of those dreams and *to cry as much as you need to*. At first you may be amazed that so many tears can come from the simple act of looking at pictures. In fact, you may fear you will *always* feel devastated when you see those photos. You won't. The depth of your pain will gradually diminish, and the length of time you experience pain after looking at pictures will shorten. You may never be able to look at pictures of your child without *some* lingering sense of loss, but once you have cleansed your grief by embracing it, your heart will feel lighter and more whole.

Three other emotions are also part of grief: anger, anxiety, and envy. Recognizing these feelings as normal can help tremendously. We need not add to our difficulties by feeling guilty for having them or by thinking we should not let others see them. In fact, sharing them with others can greatly diminish their power to prevent us from releasing our dreams.

We may be angry at our child for causing us grief; at peer pressure for dragging our child into drugs; at our ex-spouse for failing to provide support; and at myriad other factors we believe contributed to our situation.

Anxiety results from the uncertainty of not knowing what the future holds. It is, of course, hard not to be anxious, but in the absence of a crystal ball we all have to find a way to tolerate waiting for future events to unfold.

And although we don't want to admit it, we often envy those parents whose lives are perfectly content because their children turned out "okay." What did they do to deserve their good luck? Until we let go of our lost dreams, we can be caught in the envy of those whose dreams were fulfilled.

Using Our Grief to Make a Difference in the World

Parents whose children are accused of heinous or highly publicized crimes are undoubtedly in profound emotional pain. As a *Los Angeles Times* article pointed out, "They are thrust into a sordid kind of limelight, besieged by police and reporters, blamed for their errant child's behavior, ostracized by friends and neighbors, or even sued by the victim's parents."

Yet often these parents turn their grief and tragedy into efforts to change society. Jack and JoAnn Hinckley were devastated when their son, John, nearly assassinated President Reagan in 1981. "I am the cause of John's tragedy," Jack Hinckley said in testimony during his son's 1982 trial. "I wish to God I could trade places with him right now." In an effort to make up to society for the damage done by their child, the Hinckleys sold their company and founded the American Mental Health Fund, to prevent other such tragedies through public service announcements, a free booklet on mental illness, and an 800 number that answered inquiries from over 330,000 people.

We need not be famous parents with profound pain and guilt (or have a lot of money) to work through our grief by trying to help others. There are many ways we can transform our grief and negative emotional energy into something more positive, bringing light into the small corner of the world where we live.

If your grief is caused by guilt for not giving your children what they needed when they were young, you can transform that guilt-driven energy by helping children whose parents may not know what you have painfully learned. You can be a big brother or big sister to teenagers in trouble, tutor in a local school, work in a women's shelter, teach an illiterate adult to read, or become the friend of an AIDS patient.

Adding these activities to your life will have a threefold effect. You will get more than you give; your grief will dissipate more quickly; and you will have far less time to fret over the problems your child may be having.

A Technique For Saying Good-bye to Lost Dreams

We help release the grip grief has on our hearts when we say good-bye to our hopes and dreams one by one. The following method has been helpful in facilitating the process of releasing unfulfilled and broken dreams.

Write on separate pieces of paper all the hopes you had *and* all the pain you have experienced. Each page should contain a different item, such as, "I expected that my daughter would want to keep her baby;" "I expected my son would want to visit me;" "I hoped to share the holidays with my daughter;" or "I have spent far too much time trying to get my son to change." Make certain you cover everything you can remember that has kept you imprisoned in unreleased grief.

Next, take the pieces of paper— and the hopes and pains they represent—and let go of them in a ritual that has meaning for you. You might want to burn them and watch the paper turn to ashes, take them to an ocean or lake and toss them into the waves, or flush them down the toilet.

Each time you burn a paper, throw it away, or flush it down the toilet, say aloud a statement that affirms your desire to release that which has kept you in pain. On those papers that involve lost dreams write, "*I release my expectations that . . .*" (For example, "I release my expectation that I would share religious beliefs with my son.") On the papers that describe your pain write, "*I say good-bye to . . .*" (For example, "I say good-bye to lost sleep because of worry.)

With each paper, allow yourself to experience the healing and peace that come when you willingly give up something you have wanted but cannot have.

When that part of the "ceremony" is through, you can then welcome what you see in the future by writing on new pieces of paper— ones you will keep—the realistic hopes you can now have. Imagine how wonderful it will be to write, "I welcome the opportunity to accept my child just as she is" or, "I look forward to spending less energy worrying." You may want to write the same statement on several pieces of paper and then put those papers somewhere where you will see them every day. They can become a beacon of light out of grief.

A Comforting Picture of Peace

I want to share with you how I discovered a way to release my lost expectations and hope when I was in the midst of great pain over the situation with our son. I believe my experience illustrates what can happen when we are open to healing.

When David was forced to move out of our house for the last time, we knew that letting him go was the most loving action we could take. Yet it was extremely painful to force a child to leave knowing he was poorly prepared to face the trials ahead of him. That night I was unable to sleep and went into my husband's study hoping to find some measure of comfort.

To understand what happened, you need to know that during that time of my life, and even sometimes now, I found it helpful to talk out loud when I was trying to sort through a problem. Because I am fairly verbal, hearing the words could give me insights I might not have discovered if I processed my thoughts internally.

On the door of the study was a poster of a gentle stream high in the Sierras far above the timberline. I happened to be looking at the picture as I said out loud, with great sobs, "If there is a God, please grant me the peace I so desperately want. I have done everything I can, and yet my grief seems more than I can bear."

Almost immediately I felt calmer and in a quiet, soothing voice I said, "You are seated on a stone next to the stream. Lying at your side is an invisible rope which you have just let go of. The rope is of infinite length and has been used by you and David to manipulate one another. The other end of it is still being held by David, who has started down the mountain and is out of view. Your letting go of the rope indicates you are willing to trust your son to find his own path, just as you are learning to find your own." Then I added, "Bob is standing next to the stream and he has also dropped his end of a rope that has connected him with David. Your son will find his own path because you have both been willing to let him go."

Where did that healing wisdom come from? It does not matter whether God really spoke through me or whether the words I said were simply my own inner wisdom expressing itself in a metaphor I could understand. What matters is that I experienced a sense of peace I could not have imagined possible earlier that day.

There is a footnote to this story. Thanksgiving came two months later and for many reasons we chose not to invite our son for dinner. His absence created a hole in the fabric of our family and reminded me of the deep pain I had felt earlier. As I wondered how I could get through the day without being constantly reminded of the fact that David was spending Thanksgiving alone, I decided to go into the study and look again at the picture of the mountain stream. Immediately I felt comforted as the peace I had experienced earlier returned to soothe my heart.

The Need to Forgive

Geraldine was one the most interesting parents I interviewed. Her situation represents the complexity of the healing process and demonstrates that dealing with Velcro issues and grieving are not always enough to heal relationships. Forgiveness is often the missing ingredient.

> *Geraldine's father and mother were both alcoholics. Her father was a highly successful businessman before he died at the age of fifty. Geraldine describes her mother as "a cold woman for whom appearances meant everything: she never touched me because I might break her long fingernails." To escape the situation at home, she entered a convent. When she left ten years later, she had an automobile accident that led to an addiction to pain killers, and soon she was on her way to years of drug and alcohol abuse.*
>
> *She married and had three daughters: Becky, now twenty-seven, Laura, twenty-four, and Julia, twenty-one. After her divorce she was married twice more before entering a lesbian relationship, which has also ended. All the men in her life were addicts of either drugs or alcohol.*
>
> *Modeling her parenting on her mother's example, she says that her daughters were taught to be charming and well mannered: she had them practice etiquette during tea time with their dolls. She was a "smiling mom" and believed that "if I could impress you with what was on the outside, I thought I had it together."*
>
> *Today, however, her beautiful smile is much more congruent with what is going on inside her. And she has shed many tears, in and out of therapy, during her long recovery process, grieving over a lifetime of troubles she has had a hand in creating.*
>
> *Geraldine says her relationship with her children is currently "on hold, as though they are on a shelf," adding that she*

"doesn't feel anything for them." From her perspective, this stance may have been necessary in order to stay clean and get her life in order. Yet she is clearly pained in not seeing her children, especially because she and Becky had been "best friends."

Since sobriety and honesty are Geraldine's primary goals, she has attempted to make amends with her children and let them know she is aware of the mistakes she made when raising them. But since her latest recovery from a relapse, she says her daughters "don't want to hear what I'm going through." She does not think things will get better, expecting "history will repeat itself," since she has not seen her own mother for fifteen years.

Yet history does not have to repeat itself. Just because Geraldine broke off contact with her mother does not mean that her daughters will necessarily continue to reject her. They may just have a problem being with her at this time because she is preoccupied with her recovery process, which has been, in a sense, her Velcro issue.

In fact, when discussing the last time she had dinner with Laura (many months before), Geraldine said she had talked about herself almost the entire evening. At the end of the conversation Laura commented that her mother had never inquired into what was happening in her daughter's life. Ironically, Geraldine's focus on making an inventory of her mistakes and on attempting to make amends may be her current contribution to the rift with her daughters.

It is probably true that her daughters were raised with an emphasis on appearances, but they also enjoyed childhood. There was fun and laughter; they saw Geraldine as a good mom. It is not surprising that they balk when she tries to get them to see her mistakes, to recognize she could have done better, to forgive her. She thinks they don't want to forgive her because that would be admitting everything wasn't fun and laughter.

The real issue, of course, is not whether her daughters experienced their childhoods as she believes they "should"—if only they could see through the lens of her self-examination. Rather, the real issue and a more significant stumbling block to a better relationship with her daughters is her reluctance to forgive herself. It can seem impossible, of course, to forgive oneself when one's life appears to have been a series of major mistakes. Yet it is not only possible, it is essential, that Geraldine forgive herself; not only for the sake of a potentially healed relationship with her daughters, but for her own peace of mind.

When we insist that *our* particular sins are too great for us to forgive or that we must maintain our resentment against those who did us wrong (so that our pain will not be "meaningless"), we might consider the story of Edith Eva Eger. Edith is a former ballerina whose parents were killed in a Nazi concentration camp. Her career as a dancer was ended when her back was broken by a guard in the camp. Although her life is filled with frequent flashbacks to the horrors of those days, she says that she has no time to hate. She is convinced that if she still hated today she would continue to be in prison, giving Hitler and Mengele their posthumous victories. If she hated, they would still be in charge of her life, not her.

Just as an unwillingness to grieve our lost dreams can prevent sunshine from entering our lives, the heart that cannot forgive others holds it own self hostage. And there is only so long we can continue saying, *"mea culpa, mea culpa,"* and refuse to forgive ourselves.

What Is Forgiveness?

Forgiveness is one of the most misunderstood essential qualities of the human spirit. Perhaps this is because there are really three kinds of forgiveness, each with its own peculiar characteristics, and we confuse one with the other. For example, one kind of forgiveness is that which God is said to bestow through an act of grace; another is granted by the state in the form of official pardons; and still another is the forgiveness humans try to achieve with one another.

I can't speak authoritatively on what God will or will not forgive, and pardons are not ours to grant. However, I can talk about the last kind of forgiveness, that which heals the one doing the forgiving and which can also lead to healing for the one being forgiven.

Some of our difficulty with forgiveness seems to stem from our belief that forgiveness means *forgetting* and that forgiveness acts as an *excuse* for one's behavior. When someone says "I'm sorry," we frequently respond, "Oh, forget it." In fact, the word "amnesty" comes from "amnesia"—to forget. So when we forgive someone, we may assume that we should act as though nothing has happened. Perhaps that is what God's kind of forgiveness means.

Human forgiveness, however, does not mean forgetting. It does not negate the consequences for the person we forgive. And it does not mean that we insist on reconciliation with the person who has injured us. All it requires of us is that we release the demands, expectations, and conditions we place on other people (and on ourselves) that they (we) should *be someone* that they (we) did not know how to be, or to *do something* that they (we) did not know how to do.

Patty McConnell discusses the necessity for the kind of forgiv-

ing that parents (and children) need to do for one another in her book
A Workbook for Healing, which was excerpted and adapted in *Mothering
Magazine.* Recognizing that we sometimes feel we cannot forgive because of the depth of a wound, she suggests that those who are
wounded ask themselves whether they "want to get well or get
even." "Not to forgive," she says, "grafts you to the past like a flower-
ing branch to a disfigured tree. Not to forgive isolates us through judgments and self-righteousness . . . Forgiveness, however, unifies and
heals. When you forgive, you let go of separateness, anger, guilt, loss,
and other persistent tormentors. Freeing others, you free yourself."

Let me add that we contribute to much-needed peace in the
world when we learn to accept and forgive those with whom we disagree. After all, how can we expect societies to be understanding and
tolerant of others if we ourselves cannot forgive those closest to us?

Forgiving Others

There is no question but that all of our parents failed us, in one way
or another, when we were children, and that we have, likewise, failed
our children. For both parent and child, dealing with those failures
can sometimes require a good dose of forgiving.

In 1968, when David was just five years old, the idea that I might
need to forgive him, or he might need to forgive me, had not yet crossed
my mind. But that was the year Henry T. Close wrote some words of wisdom in *Voices* that I would read years later, at a time when I needed to address the issue of forgiveness. A colleague had copied his words and the
Xeroxed paper was a kind friend to my broken dreams.

Close wrote that no parent is ever adequate for the job of being
a parent. No parent ever has enough love, or wisdom, or maturity or
whatever to succeed one hundred percent of the time. And so it is
necessary for us to forgive our parents and our children not for their
sake, but for ours. We cannot afford to hold onto grudges while we
wait for them to forgive us any more than they can afford to wait for us
to forgive them.

There Is Usually Someone We Need to Forgive

The following statements illustrate the variety of people disappointed parents may hold grudges against, viewing them as wholly or
partially responsible for their child's current problems or for the parent's
pain. In interviews with parents and conversations with my clients, these
statements were always preceded by the words, "I resent . . ." or, if the
individual had worked through the issue and let go with forgiveness,
"I used to resent . . ."

- " . . . my son-in-law for deserting my daughter when she became pregnant."
- ". . . the neighborhood gang that led our child to drugs and
  crime."
- ". . . my boyfriend for molesting my daughter."
- ". . . my spouse for having affairs that led to the breakup of our
  marriage."
- ". . . my father for being abusive and failing to teach me how
  to trust men."
- ". . . my wife, because she didn't want a girl and let our daughter believe that girls are inferior."
- ". . . my daughter for putting me through the pain of watching
  her addiction."
- ". . . my second wife for not getting along with the daughter
  from my first marriage."
- ". . . my son for being a pathological liar whose immaturity has
  caused us a great deal of pain and expense in trying to get him
  straightened out."
- ". . . my wife for being very possessive of the biological child
  in the family and stricter with our adopted children."

When to Forgive Others

At what point in dealing with resentments is it time to let them
go? If you have not yet recognized and worked through at least some
of your anger toward a person you think you "should" forgive, an attempt to forgive at this point may be premature. In fact, lightly skip-
ping over resentments can prevent you from knowing exactly what it
is that you need to forgive. You may end up simply hiding your resentment under the rug. Forgiveness in such cases often feels "phony" and
does not lead to genuine harmony and peace. This can certainly happen
when you are dealing with very serious behaviors, such as sexual abuse
by your ex-husband. There is a lot of work you will need to do before you
can let go of your hurt enough to even see him as a person with frailties,
as one who did not know how to be a responsible parent.

However, you can delay healing by thinking you have to deal
with every scrap of negative emotion before you can even *begin* to forgive. And be aware that you may have to repeat these exercises more
than once before you experience complete release of resentment. I
found it necessary to forgive David—and myself—many times. Each
occasion provided release from my pain as it removed one more piece
of the hurt that kept me focused on my disappointment that things

didn't turn out as I wanted them to. It has been several years since I last felt the need to forgive either of us, which is an indication of how well I am doing. Yet I imagine it is possible I may feel the need to forgive one of us if something else comes up in the future.

A Few Techniques for Forgiving Others

Patty McConnell offers the following method for restoring inner harmony by forgiving others. She recommends you use it as is or adapt it to suit your needs.

- Take a pencil and a notebook to a comfortable place where you'll be uninterrupted. Sit quietly for a few minutes.
- When you feel relaxed, complete the following statement. *Today, for my own well-being, I choose to forgive these people:* (List them.)
- Then read that statement and the names out loud, followed by: *I let go of these incidents, and my reaction to them, and I wish the people I have named sincere goodwill. If an individual is deceased, I wish him or her eternal peace. In doing so, I release myself from the past and its pain. The people and incidents I have forgiven no longer have power over me.*

Her approach is slightly different from the following method for forgiveness I have used with myself and my clients, although both can be highly effective. The attitude involved in this exercise is the willingness to take responsibility for oneself and to allow others to take responsibility for themselves. From this perspective *forgiveness is a decision to no longer hold onto pain caused by the wrongs of others or by circumstances over which you had no control.*

You can either write this exercise on a piece of paper or place a chair in front of you and imagine that the person you want to forgive is sitting there. See him or her as clearly as possible. Then go through the following steps, either to yourself or out loud, saying:

1. "You said or did _____, while I would have preferred you had said or done _____. I have let myself be tied to negative feelings when I think of what you did or did not do. And I have held onto my demand that you should have said or done something different. I choose to let go of the tension and hurt that accompanies my memory of what you said or did."
2. "Therefore, I cancel all demands, expectations, and conditions that you do or say _____. You are totally responsible for your own actions and deeds."

3. "I now send my love [or, if that word is too strong for you, my acceptance] out to you as a human being just as you were and are now."

After this part of the exercise, close your eyes and imagine that your love or acceptance, without conditions, demands or expectations, is going out to the other person. Take your time. Become aware of how your body feels and whether you are holding on or still demanding that the person be different from the way he or she was, or is. If you do not feel release, then repeat the process again.

Incidentally, you will probably need to go through the process for many different resentments you hold against another person. The human mind finds it almost impossible to grant a blanket forgiveness. Each incident must be processed separately. However, forgiveness is like the untangling of scraps of yarn and string that have been tightly bunched together. At first it's hard to untangle a single strand, but with persistence the first piece can be removed. And then another. And another. Eventually it becomes easier and easier to pull the pieces apart, and the last ones can be removed with almost no effort at all.

The idea that by *choosing* not to feel badly you can actually prevent yourself from *feeling* badly may be a new concept for you. After all, when someone is mean-spirited and says something she knows is hurtful, you are likely to feel hurt at the time. However, in looking back on the situation later, you can distance yourself from your painful reaction by choosing to let go of your *insistence* (the demands, expectations and conditions you place on her) that she must be kind-hearted. The power of this approach is that it allows you to be in charge of how you react to what others do or say. You can decide how you will react even when others fail to meet your expectations, no matter how reasonable those expectations may appear.

Forgiving Ourselves

Some parents don't spend any time analyzing what they did wrong in raising their child, even though their child's current values and lifestyle may be not only different than theirs but even, from the parent's point of view, undesirable and destructive. They do not hold themselves responsible for what he does, although others may insist the parents have to accept blame for how their child turned out. These parents may or may not recognize their parenting mistakes, but they are able to leave the past alone and can separate their own value and success in life from that of their child, giving him plenty of room to make his own mistakes.

Other disappointed parents don't experience a need to forgive themselves because they believe genetic factors, such as dyslexia and attention deficit disorder, were primary influences on the development of their child's problems. Some parents, usually fathers, don't hold themselves responsible for their children's problems because they were not active in the daily care of their children, although they don't necessarily blame the other parent. And if the spouse was mentally ill, a parent may excuse herself in the belief that the ill partner influenced the children negatively more than she did.

Even when parents accept responsibility for the contribution they made to their child's current problems and lifestyle choices, they don't necessarily use that self-awareness as a whip to continue berating themselves for what they didn't know how to do better. For example, one mother of three sons, all of whom have difficulties in maintaining relationships, felt badly for years that she didn't "do a better job" as a parent. One day, however, she had the clear awareness that she had done the very best she could after her husband died when their youngest was only three. With that insight she was able to let her guilt dissipate. She could then stop being concerned over things like the length of her son's hair and "give up taking responsibility for how things turned out."

Most parents disappointed in their adult children regret something they did or did not do when their child was young. What they do with that regret can have a profound effect on whether they are able to build an adult-to-adult relationship with their child or remain mired in remorse and self-recrimination.

A Step-mother Who Needed to Forgive Herself

When Patricia married Doug sixteen years ago, his son, Colin, now twenty-two, stayed with Doug's former wife but came to visit every weekend. There were hints of Colin's future difficulties even then, when Colin would refuse to stack blocks, determined not be structured. So Patricia's contribution toward Colin's life is not straightforward, as it might have been if she weren't a stepparent and if he hadn't always seemed to be a "different" kind of child. Nevertheless, Colin's rough entry into adulthood illustrates how a parent can come to terms with her role in The Parenting Game.

In my interviews with parents I begin by asking some standard questions about such things as where the child lives and what his education has been. On my interview form I notice Colin's career choice is "undefined;" marital status is "living with woman who has a five-year-old child;" and grade average is "terrible." After getting this standard information, I asked his parents to describe Colin. The first of my notes says, "Dropped out of high school as sophomore; very self-willed; gifted; inquisitive but makes judgments prematurely and decisions too far-ranging; egocentric; can be very loving and caring and sharing but more often gets absorbed in the flow of his life; very impulsive; very, very excitement/adrenaline oriented."

Colin lived with his mother until he was ten and then with Patricia and Doug for a few years, back again to his mother's where he eventually ran away, acted out in erratic behavior, used crack, and later participated in drug dependency programs with only moderate success. To get into the Navy he had to be sober, and that, apparently, was the incentive he needed to get off drugs completely. And since structure has always been a problem for him, boot camp was good training. Colin has been sober now for two years and uses twelve-step meetings as a resource when life gets chaotic. However, Patricia doesn't think he's working the steps, and believes he resists dealing with important issues in his life. For example, he insists that he wasn't responsible for a car accident, although there were witnesses to the contrary, and that he's not liable for the judgment against him because he wasn't served papers directly. He is in debt to many people, including his parents, and is unlikely to pay what he owes.

As Patricia looks back on Colin's life, she realizes that she and Doug have to accept their fair share of responsibility for what has happened. For example, as members of the sixties generation they both used marijuana and alcohol, although they did not use them in front of either Colin or Patricia's daughter Sarah when the children were young. But Patricia and Doug allowed themselves to get into a fast crowd in their upwardly mobile community and had to declare bankruptcy. Eventually Patricia joined AA and has worked hard to stay off alcohol and drugs, especially the codeine she became addicted to when she had migraines.

Patricia's story, like the tales of many parents, has many more facets than I've presented here. However, even this much can give you a sense of what she was responding to when she made an inventory one day of twenty things Colin did that made her angry. To her surprise, nineteen of them reflected her need to control. Consequently, even though Patricia knew it was necessary that she forgive her son for the turmoil *he* caused the family, she came to see that she needed to forgive *herself* for the way in which she added to those conflicts.

Guilt Monkeys Cling to Our Backs

If you were to make a list of what bothered you about your child, would you be like Patricia and discover that you, too, contributed to the family conflict more than you wish you had? If you are like most people, you probably would. We all carry on our backs monkeys of one size or another. These pesky creatures, who answer to the name of Guilt, whisper in our ears and tell us what we've done wrong, where we've missed, how things would have turned out differently if only we had done such-and-such. They remind us in a hundred ways that we were not the perfect parents we "should" have been. And listening to them we kick ourselves for making mistakes we believe contribute to our child's poor choices as an adult.

Here are a few examples of the guilt-monkeys that have pestered some of the parents I've known:

- "Not protecting my daughter from the craziness of her mother even though I knew the children were at points frightened of her."

- "Not being able to help my daughters work through the grief of their brother's death."

- "Not noticing my son's drug use was a cry for help because I was 'liberal' and 'experimenting' was okay."

- "Manipulating the situation so my stepson, who was only six and acting out his reaction to his parents' breakup, would want to go back with his mother rather than stay with me."

- "Not recognizing my grandchildren were neglected and deprived because their parents had fancy cars and good jobs."

- "Being unable to realize my daughter was molested for ten years by her stepfather."

- "Not divorcing when I first knew love had gone, but waiting until after the fighting was well under way."

- "Having an affair that broke up our marriage."

A Balanced Perspective is Needed

The next section contains an exercise on self-forgiveness that has brought comfort and peace to many people. However, before attempting to forgive ourselves, it is imperative we remember that *our faults are only part of who we are.* We were neither all "good" nor all "bad," but a combination of many skills and missteps. Yet sometimes we view our faults as though they are buckets filled with black coal. The good things we did are represented by a small pile of gold. When we place the coal and gold on a balance scale, the coal will obviously outweigh the gold.

If we wish to use a balance scale to determine how much forgiveness we will require in order to lessen the guilt we feel, we need to first make a list of *everything* we did as parents, the positive qualities as well as those times we missed the boat. And then we need to weigh them against each other by using the same measuring scale!

The following are some of the ways in which parents (most of whom were disappointed in a child) have acknowledged their positive qualities, while at the same time not being blind to parenting decisions and attitudes that weren't as positive.

- "I talked with my children; they could always come to me with their problems."
- "We gave our children a lot of latitude to grow and didn't put them on a tight chain, even though problems with cocaine may have gone too far because of that."
- "Our children knew they were loved."
- "We challenged them intellectually."
- "We took vacations together."
- "We instilled high standards of respect for family, religious values, and tolerance."
- "I didn't watch much TV because I wanted to be a good example to my children; instead I read or kept busy with other projects."
- "I don't give 'advice.' I only offer my opinions, thoughts, and feelings and my children can do with it what they want."
- "I spent a lot of time with my children despite a busy schedule and having children spread between three marriages."

An Exercise for Forgiveness of Oneself

There are only two requirements if people wish to forgive themselves. One is the courage to cut away the guilt that binds them to the past. The other is learning how.

Assuming that you have the willingness to learn, here is a proven method to let go of the heavy weight of guilt you have been carrying for many years. It is quite similar to the forgiveness approach given earlier.

Remember something you did (or failed to do) that now causes you to feel badly when you think of how your child has turned out. Imagine yourself at that time in your life when you made decisions you now regret. What was it that you did that you now wish you had not done (or that you failed to do)? What were your intentions in doing what you did (or failed to do)?

Did you wake up in the morning and deliberately decide to mess up your life or the life of your child? Did you know that other choices were *better* but you wanted to do something you *knew* would be dumb? Of course not. Just as today you try to do the best you know how, you attempted then to do the best you could. You did not *plan* to make poor choices. Unfortunately, when you think about who you were back then, you may berate yourself for not making better choices. So now is the time to make friends with that younger part of yourself, forgiving him or her for making mistakes you later regretted making.

Imagine that you, as the person you are today, are sitting in a chair looking at the person you were when you made the choices you wish you hadn't made. As you look objectively at that younger person, you can see how much you didn't know, how much you still had to learn. So now look at your younger self and say slowly and compassionately: "For a long time I have expected you to make choices you did not know how to make and do things you did not know how to do. For a long time I have wanted you to be different from who you were. Now I am willing to remove the conditions I placed on you to be someone you could not be at the time. I remove the conditions I placed on you to be someone you could not be at the time. I remove the demands and expectations that have kept me from accepting you. My love and affection go out to you just as you are."

Feel love flowing from you to the younger person you still carry inside, the one who was doing the best he or she could do at the time mistakes were made. Let that love flow through every part of your body. Feel the release of tension that comes from forgiveness.

Chapter 8

Letting Go With Love

Reaching this final stage on the path to healing is like discovering, after a strenuous hike, that the path near the top of the mountain is gentler than we had expected. The tasks we need to accomplish here, while still challenging, are so much easier now that we have moved through the other stages. We are finally prepared to let go with love. An adult-to-adult relationship—and peace of mind—is right around the corner.

As pointed out earlier, letting go involves the process of transferring responsibility for our child's life from *us* to *them*. We move our focus from that of being *parents* to that of being *peers*. In letting go we de-emphasize the parent-child aspect of our relationship, although our family connection will always be part of the equation.

This process of letting go involves learning to treat our children as adults, just as we treat our friends as adults. In fact, an ideal adult-to-adult relationship with our children can be modeled on the ideals of friendship.

While our friends probably share most of our values and lifestyles, many of us have at least a few friends whose views on life are quite different from ours. We may not see these people on a daily basis, but when we are together we enjoy their company and don't try to talk them into being other than who they are, or require them to live out our dreams or fulfill an arbitrary set of expectations. We can have equally satisfying relationships with adult children who are also out of sync with us in some way.

If we've known a friend since childhood, we will, of course, share more memories with that person, but part of what makes friendships work is the attention that is given to the *present* rather than the past or future. Realizing this can encourage us to work toward keeping our interactions with our children more centered in the here and now. And by focusing on what is happening today, we allow both ourselves and our child to evolve into the people we want to be tomorrow, rather than constricting our perceptions by how we viewed one another in the past.

A bit of practice will be needed before these new behaviors become second nature. It will take time, just as it has taken time to work our way through the other stages. Yet our efforts will be rewarded when we accept our child just as he is, in the same way we accept our friends just as they are.

Incidentally, all of the suggestions for letting go with love apply not only to those children in whom we are disappointed in some way but to all our other children as well.

Being a Friend to Our Child

What we expect from our friends we should be able to expect from our adult children—and what our friends expect from us, our children should be able to expect from us. It's a two-way street.

If it is impossible, however, for you to have any real connection with your child no matter how hard you try, or if your child has died, your letting go with love will need to involve the process of closure, which is discussed in the next chapter. Nevertheless, understanding the principles that guide friendships can provide the underpinning for that kind of healing as well.

The following are seven expectations we have of our friends. Notice "friends" can refer to adult children and "they" and "them" can refer to either friends or adult children.

We expect our friends to be there when we need them, if possible.

If our daughter needs to borrow our car because hers is in the shop, it's not unreasonable for us to loan her ours—if we can afford to spare it. If we need a bedroom painted and our son knows how to paint, it is not unreasonable to ask whether he would be willing to help us out—provided he can spare the time and wants to help in that particular project. We often have a *quid pro quo* with our friends, helping each other in times of need, and we can work toward that arrangement with our children.

Our reciprocity with friends recognizes their right to decide what *they* will do with their time, money, and energy. And they respect *our* right to make decisions concerning what we will do. With our children, however, a major stumbling block to letting go can be our assumption that we are somehow required to respond to our child's every request if we are going to be loving parents. Likewise, we can assume our children will always be there for us. Then when they don't respond as we would like (in everything from the number of phone calls to the gifts they give), our hurt response can leave them feeling guilty. And when we don't respond as *they* would like, *we* feel guilty. Yet nowhere is it written that parents must loan their child a car just because she asks for it. Nowhere is it written that children must jump whenever their parents need help or feel a bit lonely.

We do not have the right to demand anything from our children, not even love. We can *ask*. We cannot *demand*. When we demand that our child act in a certain way or have a particular value (a demand we may express outwardly or simply feel inside), we attempt to deny them their right to decide how they will spend their time, money, or energy. We deny them their right to think for themselves.

One way you can avoid feeling upset and hurt when your child has not responded to your wishes is to notice what it is that you wanted him to say or do. Then make a statement to yourself of what you would have *preferred* him to say or do. The operative word is "prefer." Take my case as an example.

I would like David to keep us informed of what he is doing and not wait for us to drive seven hundred miles to see him. If I consider my desire for closer contact as an expectation that he *must* or *should* think of us more often, I will experience a deep sense of disappointment. If he almost never gets in touch with us except when he wants something from us, it can seem almost as though he has disobeyed a law from the center of the universe, or wherever the source of "musts" and "shoulds" is located. If, however, I say that, "I prefer that David give our family more consideration and wish he would stay in touch more often," I do not have nearly as strong of a reaction. The operative word here is "prefer." Unlike "should," "must," and "ought to," which are words of demand, *prefer* implies that the other person has the right—and responsibility—to decide what he will do.

We expect our friends to respect our privacy, just as we respect theirs.

A parent I interviewed told me that she has certain rules for herself about how she will relate to her four grown children. For instance, she said, "We always call before going to our children's houses. To do otherwise would be to treat them as though we had a right, just because we are their parents, to expect them to be there for us." Perhaps you feel perfectly content having friends drop in to visit, whether or not your house is a disaster zone. Your children may share your philosophy. But if you wouldn't want *your* friends (and especially not your own parents or in-laws) to drop in unannounced, don't expect your children to be thrilled when you do it.

The same goes for asking our children how much they are making or how much they have spent on some item we are sure is beyond the range of their budget. Curiosity can kill a cat, and if we aren't careful, it can also screw up perfectly good relationships.

We expect our friends to accept us as we are, including our imperfections, and we accept them as they are. We take pleasure in sharing the victories and defeats that are an inevitable part of every person's life.

A major advantage of letting go is the relief of no longer needing to pretend that we are perfect parents, or perfect people. We no longer have to work so hard to demonstrate that we love our child unconditionally, as many parents assume they must. On second thought, perhaps parents are asked to *love* their children unconditionally, but they certainly aren't required to *like* them unconditionally.

Our children aren't required to like us, either. They don't need to enjoy our music or friends or opinions. We need not be offended if they are bored at our parties, or if we are bored at theirs and find the background music much too loud for our taste. Having a comfortable relationship doesn't mean we abandon our values and personal tastes or suspend our judgment. We only need to be willing to view each other with compassion, without illusions or expectations.

Once we're willing to accept each other just as we are, we can stop being defensive. Our children can stop being defensive as well. We can learn to be satisfied with a brief visit from our children during which we are genuinely comfortable in each other's presence, rather than insist on doing things together because that is what we believe good parents and their good adult children are *supposed* to do.

Remember that we can be "right" or we can have a relationship of respect and trust. *We can't have both.*

We expect our friends to take responsibility for their own actions. We expect them to have the capacity to manage their own affairs without relying unnecessarily on support or direction from us.

It is a basic assumption in friendship that friends will accept the consequences of their actions. Imagine, for example, that a group of our friends decides to meet at a new restaurant and that one of the couples had the date wrong, or hadn't paid attention to a noise in the car's engine and it wouldn't start when they were ready to leave, or through some other mistake on their part fails to join us. We will be disappointed they weren't there to join in the fun, but we won't give it much thought. Certainly we don't scold them for all the other times they've made similar mistakes. We don't take on the responsibility of seeing to it that they don't make that mistake again.

Parents, however, can respond to adult children who make such errors by suggesting they be sure to get the date right the next time, by encouraging them to get their car in good working order, or in some way offering advice that is intended to help them be more "responsible." This is especially true if we believe a major problem for them is their lack of maturity.

But there is probably no greater example of the difference between how some parents view their friends and how they view their adult children than in the arena of personal finances. Consider what we would do if we learned that our friends over-extended themselves financially. We would not offer to pay their bills but would assume that they will somehow work out a responsible way to meet their responsibilities. Frequently, however, we do not apply that same philosophy to our grown child, even when, perhaps especially when, our child fails to demonstrate a willingness or ability to handle money responsibly.

We may say we want our child to learn the consequences of his choices, but we often short-circuit his opportunity for learning this essential lesson. Let's say our son chooses to drive without insurance and has an accident. What do we do? Do we help him out because, poor thing, the accident wasn't entirely his fault? Or do we allow him to discover, through long months of paying his fair share, that insurance is not a luxury but one of those necessities that needs to be paid before he buys a new tape player? There is a consequence to our child's choices, including his decision to buy expensive electronic equipment rather than buy insurance or pay the rent on time.

We expect to share our values, worries, and enthusiasms with our friends and expect they will share theirs, even though we may not agree with one another.
Friends' ideas about life are often different from ours. Nevertheless, we feel enriched when we share our beliefs and ideals, our likes and dislikes, our fears and wishes with one another. We can also enjoy sharing with our children if we don't take the occasion as an opportunity to bend them to our way of thinking.

Incidentally, we cannot assume, just because our children have grown up in our home, that they know our deepest ideals, or the important events that shaped our lives, or the stories of those from whom we came. Yet if we don't pass on our values and family history to future generations, who will? In fact, this may be a better time for your children to know about you than when they were growing up. You've learned some things you didn't know before.

If you think you're ready to share openly who you are and what you hold as a basic philosophy of life, without using your views as a bully pulpit, you may want both to talk with your child directly and to express your ideas through the writing of what is called an "ethical will." These documents or statements of philosophy can include such things as important lessons you've learned in life, some scriptural passages of particular significance, mistakes that you have made, and things for which you ask forgiveness. Your children may be surprised at how highly you value certain things. You may be surprised to learn that your children did not know how strongly you felt about those things.

One of the fathers whom I interviewed for this book prepared his own kind of ethical will as a gift to his adult children for Christmas. It is a wonderful example of what can happen when we take the time and effort to communicate with our children. His gift is included in the Appendix.

We expect our friends will respect our desire not to discuss certain topics and we allow our friends to keep some topics off-limits.

If you and your child have diametrically opposing views on certain issues, such as abortion, it is understandable that talking about them is not going to change either of your minds. If either of you insists on bringing up the subject, you will both continue to feel you are getting nowhere. Avoiding such pointless discussions only makes good sense.

If there are topics that cause you pain, it is perfectly okay for those topics to be out of bounds until you are ready to discuss them. In fact, you can do more than *hope* that these topics won't come up; you can ask your child, directly, not to bring up subjects that have proven divisive in the past.

Similarly, if your child asks you not to discuss some topic, you must honor her request, even though you may be sorely tempted to give her one more "lesson." After all, would you force your friend to talk about something if she didn't want to? Well, maybe you might, rarely, if you had a particularly good friend who was avoiding looking at something that could cause her a great deal of grief if it weren't faced, even though it was a sensitive issue. But my observation of parents and adult children is that parents frequently insist on initiating topics they know their child doesn't want to discuss with them in the hope they can steer him away from trouble (the I'm-only-saying- this-for-your-own-good method of controlling our children).

On the other hand, in choosing to have some subjects "off limits," be careful you don't decide to avoid talking about *any* difficult issue. Some topics need lots of airing for understanding and negotiations to occur, even though they are not comfortable subjects to discuss. But there can come a time when you may realize that more talking isn't going to resolve the issue, especially one that does not require mutual agreement or negotiation but is only a ploy to get the other person to change her mind. Give yourself and your children a break.

We do not expect friends to be the only source of connection, learning, love, and nurturing in our lives.

There are two ways in which we can apply this characteristic of friendships to our relationship with an adult child.

First, unless we work at maintaining lives that are rich and rewarding apart from our role as parents, we will find it difficult to release our children.

Carolyn G. Heilbrun, a professor at Columbia University for more than thirty years, addresses the need for women to use this time of life as an opportunity "to take risks, make noise, be courageous, become unpopular." The same can be said of men. In other words, we need to design our lives so they have meaning and purpose. In an article in the *Los Angeles Times Magazine* in 1992, Heilbrun notes that at a certain age, "there is no longer time for meaningless conversations, for social events where time merely passes, where obligations no longer important are merely fulfilled. One leaves one's space to take part in something that, if ever so slightly, changes the world."

When we no longer count on friends, or children, to provide the basis for all our social needs, we not only experience a richer and fuller life, we have more to share with our friends—and with our children.

Second, we must keep reminding ourselves that our child may only be able to learn what he needs to learn *after* we have let him go. There are other sources of learning besides the home.

Consider the case of Jerry, who used drugs during most of high school, dropped out, and showed no inclination to "grow up" while he was living at home. I heard of Jerry's interesting odyssey in maturity when I interviewed his parents, John and Elizabeth. John said that when Jerry was nineteen, he sold the car his parents had given him and went to Hawaii to work and to "find himself." It didn't seem to John that his son was likely to mature when bumming around without parental control, although he and Elizabeth hadn't had much success up to that point in steering him in a different direction. In any case, there was nothing Jerry's parents could do about it.

When he returned two years later, however, they were in for a surprise. John quickly realized that the time away had been well spent. As Jerry walked into the kitchen, where a bowl of fruit was sitting on the table, he asked, "May I have a banana?" John says he knew right then that his son finally saw himself as an adult, not as a child with automatic rights to take from them whatever he wanted. Events since then have reaffirmed the value Jerry received in leaving home when he did.

Find a Metaphor that Works for You

Some parents consider children clay they must mold into a specific shape. When their children are young, that philosophy may sometimes work. However, conflict arises when the parents discover the clay has a mind of its own and resists their attempts at molding. Others see babies as cute toys designed to provide them with pleasure. Again, when their children are quite young, that philosophy may be okay for awhile, but what happens when the toys rebel and resist the role of plaything for narcissists?

The metaphoric way in which we experience our children has a great deal to do with the difficulty or ease with which we can let them go.

If you regard your children as appliances that come with a warranty and must perform as expected, you may want to discard them when they start costing a bit more to support and don't function the way you thought they should. And if you see children as cars you have carefully maintained for years and assume that their performance will reflect on how well you maintain them, you may feel especially responsible if they don't work in top condition when you sell them to someone else eighteen years later.

On the other hand, do you share the view of Erma Bombeck who sees children as kites? Throughout their childhood you keep trying to get them off the ground. You run with them until you're both breathless and still they crash. You patch them up and run again, adding a longer tail. They hit a tree and you climb up to retrieve them. You patch once more, adjusting for their growing size, and caution them about the perils of unseen wind. When they are ready to try their final flight, you let out the string with joy and sadness because you know the kite will snap the line that bound you together. But you also know the kite will fly as it was meant to fly, alone and free.

A slight modification on the kite motif is one that I saw in the home of parents I interviewed for this book. In the kitchen hung a poster of a hot air balloon with the caption, *"There's freedom in loving. To love something completely you must be able to let it go."* At the bottom of the poster she had attached the high school tassels of each of her children. She believed their basic character was set by the time they were eighteen. By then she realized she had to let them go, watch what they would make of the character she had worked to instill in them, and stand back to see where their balloons would land.

It is difficult to let go of the kite or balloon that is our child if we doubt our child's ability to steer a course away from electric wires and other obstacles waiting to snatch the unwary. But unless we keep our child tied down and imprisoned, we don't have any other choice than to let go.

All Your Children Are Equally Important

Several years ago my daughter and I paid a condolence visit to the home of friends whose son had been murdered. After the visit my daughter was very upset with me—and for good reason! I had once again talked about David more than I did about our other children. She accused me of spending more time thinking about him than I did about her or her sister and brother. I knew that in the past I had focused much of my energy on him, but I thought I was over that phase. Apparently not. As other parents have noticed, it doesn't matter how satisfied you feel with your other children, when there is one that is having trouble, that one will preoccupy your mind.

After my daughter's comment, I reflected on what happened during our visit. I realized that talking about *my* pain was an attempt to convey to my friends that I understood *their* pain in losing a child. But the situations are very different because my child is alive. My only "loss" is the loss of my expectations. I may have reached the fifth stage of healing in a number of ways, but during that visit I certainly slid back into a previous stage. I decided from then on to be more conscious of how much "air time" I would give to the subject of David or to his siblings. He deserves to be mentioned in conversations about our family, but neither more nor less than the others.

All of our children are important. They all deserve our attention.

Letting Go of Adult Children Living at Home

When we were young, we would probably have assumed that a book entitled *Boomerang Kids* (by Jean Davies Okimoto and Phyllis Jackson Stegall) was about young Australian aborigines. Today, however, that term is applied to those adults, primarily in their twenties and thirties, who either return home temporarily or postpone leaving because of economic pressure, emotional upheavals, and a reluctance to sacrifice material comfort provided by parents for financial independence. Increasingly parents are discovering that they're unprepared for the phenomena that is hitting homes across America.

Letting go doesn't mean our children can't live under our roof, only that we no longer take responsibility for their lives. However, it is very hard not to slip back into the parenting role when children return home (or don't leave home in the first place). Our guilt and parenting instincts become hooked all too easily.

The following are some of my suggestions, based on ideas from Okimoto and Stegall's book, for letting go of adult children living at home.

- Establish ground rules before allowing your child to come home. Expect the child to become a fully functioning member, to pull his own weight.

- Duplicate conditions in the real world as much as possible at home. If the child has no money, demand household chores in lieu of rent.

- Parents and children should draw up an agreement or contract that stipulates how the family will function together, such as deciding that the child will mow the lawn once a week and that there is a limit to how long she may stay.

- Once your children have jobs, they should be expected to pay rent on a gradually increasing scale.

- Just as important as allowing children to return home is being able to lock them out. Refuse to admit boomerangers who are addicted to drugs or alcohol or who abuse family members.

- Do not permit your child to live at home when there is not enough money or space.

We All Regress During Visits Home

Once you decide to treat your adult children more like friends than like offspring for whom you are responsible, you will want to put that resolve into action. What better time to do that than when your children come and visit. Right? Well, yes. But watch out. There's a fly in the ointment.

Do you remember what it was like (and perhaps still is) when you went to visit your folks? You had expectations that Mom and Dad would be there for you just like they were in the old days. In fact, part of the enjoyment of anticipating a return to your parent's home was the fun of knowing Mom would cook the dishes she knew you liked. Dad would tell his old jokes and everyone would still laugh. And even though the old days were chaotic, whenever you returned home you assumed they would continue to be the way you remembered.

Unless parents experience major changes in their children's personalities, they usually continue to relate to their children in ways they've always related. The same is true for children. They expect us to act in ways we've always acted, to think as we've always thought, to hold the values we've had for years.

The consequence of these expectations is that everyone in the family seems to regress when they get together. On the one hand, there is comfort and strength in experiencing the stability of loving relationships over the years. On the other hand, we can be so convinced that things will remain the same that we don't notice the situation is different, that members in the family have developed new attitudes and are able to handle situations they previously could not. In other words, it is very easy to live in the *past* during family get-togethers and not in the *present*. And our children can easily continue replaying the old sibling rivalries that in the past kept things stirred up.

If you have reached this last stage on the road to healing and are ready to practice letting go with love, there is, fortunately, a way out of your dilemma, an outlook that can ease the transition between old behavior and new. *Expect* your next few visits to be somewhat uncomfortable—new ways of relating are unfamiliar, and what is unfamiliar can be uncomfortable. *Expect* that your children will attempt to put you into a box—they probably still see you in the light of your old attitudes and behaviors. If you can remember that the phenomena of regression is an almost universal experience and not peculiar to your family, you will be able to smile and keep carrying on.

Tell Your Children You Love Them

Grace Walls came to see me because she was having a hard time letting go of a beloved sister dying of cancer. After the funeral, she sent me an essay she had written entitled, "The Importance of Sharing Loving Feelings." It began with a brief quote from Rainer Maria Rilke and continued with Grace's plea that people express their love before it is too late.

I close this chapter with her advice (printed with her permission), because I believe it is very important that we let our children know we love them. We should not tell them we love them in the hope that we can better manipulate and control them, but simply to let them know they are loved because they are part of the human race, and part of us. Letting them know we love them—freely and without strings attached—allows us to let them go without guilt or expectations that they meet our standards.

✦ ✧ ✦

For one human being to love another,
That is perhaps the most difficult of all our tasks
The ultimate, the last test and proof,
The work for which all other work
Is but preparation.

Loving and expressing that loving is truly one of our most important "tasks" in this life. The only things that are really worth anything ultimately in life are our caring relationships, our emotional, mental, and spiritual growth, and the work that we have accomplished. Everything else—status, wealth, fame, power, ego, etc.—is worthless.

Please, tell all those whom you love, all those whom you respect and honor, your feelings. Write those caring letters to family members and friends far away, call those people you've been meaning to call, do that kind task, say that kind word TO-DAY. Tomorrow may be too late. And you may leave a hole in the universe that only your caring and your loving could fill.

— Grace Walls

Chapter 9

Closure When Reconciliation Is Not Possible

The hardest worker may not get a promotion. The most dedicated runner may not win a race. The most ardent suitor may not win the object of his affection. Doing our best does not mean we will always get what we want.

Some disappointed parents have done all they can to mend their family rift. They stopped trying to change their son or daughter and have worked on those things that kept them overly concerned about their child's current problems. They have forgiven themselves and their child, have mourned the loss of the dreams they had for their family, and have sincerely tried to let go with love. Yet their child may still choose not to include them in his life.

Sometimes it is parents and siblings who decide to distance themselves from an adult child who is extremely disruptive to family harmony.

Laura Morgan's sister had a twenty-year history of schizophrenia, compounded by alcohol and drug abuse, a situation Laura described in a commentary she wrote for *The Los Angeles Times*. Despite years of therapy and the consistent emotional and financial support of her family, her sister became increasingly delusional and violent, striking their mother on several occasions and stealing from the family to finance her drug habit. Unable to take (or give) any more, their mother packed up and moved to the Midwest two years ago. At the same time, Laura moved and got an unlisted phone number. She and her brother told their sister not to contact them. It was time for the family to cut their losses, realizing, finally, that it was a question of survival—hers or theirs. The last that Laura heard about her sister, she was living on Skid Row. That is clearly not the happy ending any family wants for one of its members.

There is a limit to what parents can handle. Just as children have rights, parents have a right to be protected from the verbal and physical abuse of their children. Yet the decision to cut off relations with our children is not done without a great deal of anguish. Even then, *knowing we are doing the right thing in distancing ourselves from our child does not take away the pain.*

In some families parents do not have a chance for reconciliation, even if they have moved through all the stages on their path of healing. Their child may have left home years ago and disappeared, offering them no opportunity to work things through. Or their child may have died from an accident, homicide, suicide, or sudden illness before they had time to heal a torn relationship.

Not all situations that appear nonreconcilable, of course, will remain that way. Ivy, a woman I interviewed, told me that she and her husband, George, had spent many sleepless nights worrying about their only child, Ben. They had once given up hope that he would turn his life around. Their son was a heavy drug abuser who had alienated himself from his parents until, in his mid-forties, he had a child of his own. Apparently at the prodding of his wife, he sent pictures of his baby, a grandchild Ivy and George hadn't seen. The letter accompanying the picture of smiling parents and offspring stated that he now realized what it meant to have a child, adding something about how much his parents had meant to him. The new relationship is still tenuous, although there is hope it can be further repaired. Nevertheless, while Ivy and George can *now* breath a little easier, at one point they had to accept, for their own peace of mind, that their child was alienated from them and that, very possibly, they would never see him again.

Unless your child has died or is completely incapacitated, there is always the *possibility* of reconciliation. But *counting* on that possibility can prevent you from ever releasing your pain and really getting on with your life.

Closure means "closing or being closed; a finish; end; conclusion." In the case of broken relationships, it is, as a friend of mine said, suturing a wound so that it can heal. Closure does not mean you write off your child forever. Instead, it is the willingness to gently close a door to the past, allowing the possibility of opening new doors for reconciliation in the future.

Stumbling Blocks to Closure

Why do the doors that need to be closed to broken relationships remain open, the wounds unsutured? There are many reasons, of course, but two common ones are the context in which we hold our pain and the way in which we expect ourselves to be judged as parents.

Defining Ourselves by Our Pain

We all know people who describe problems in their life as though their problems, pains, and sorrows are the only things worth knowing about them. My friend, Wini Pyle, however, is very different. Happening to call while I was writing this chapter, she told me that "different parts of my life are functioning at different levels." Her body isn't doing as well as she would like, her love life and spiritual life are great, her job is still rewarding. *And* she also feels sad, sometimes, because her only daughter has not been in contact with her for two years and will not even give her a phone number where she can be reached.

Wini told me that every day she releases her child, opening the door to the possibility that her daughter may choose to write her or otherwise reopen the relationship. In the meantime, my friend provides a wonderful illustration of the way in which we can view alienation from a child in a healthy way.

Certainly it is healthy to acknowledge our loss and pain from time to time. Yet we must also remind ourselves that that relationship is only *part* of who we are. There are other aspects to us as well. We do not need to display our pain like a giant sign across our chest, as Hester Prynne is compelled to do in *The Scarlet Letter*.

Defining Our Worth by How Our Children Turn Out

Some parents are unable to close the door on irreconcilable differences with their adult children because of the standards by which they believe others will judge them. These standards include the expectation that they, alone, are held accountable for their family's rift, as though they should have been able to control *both* sides of that relationship. They expect they will be found worthless if their child is not reconciled with them, or if he doesn't turn out the way they, and possibly others, might wish.

Many parents won't let go of their child—and won't allow their wounds to heal—because they believe their best wasn't good enough and because they hope, in some vague way, that by holding on they can somehow make up for past limitations. When I talk with these parents, I tell them about the reports that have been gathered of people who have had "near-death experiences." I share with them my fascination in one particular aspect of "NDEs" as they are called. This is the account given by those individuals who have met a "being of light" or "wise being" as they waver between life and death.

If this "being" talks to the person only two questions are asked. One is, "Did you love?" The other, "Did you learn?" Notice that the questions are not: "Were you a good parent?" "How many possessions did you accumulate?" or "What side of the abortion issue were you on?"

NDEs are mysterious phenomena. There are those who accept them as evidence of life on the other side of death and those who say they're nothing more than hallucinations induced by trauma. Whatever the truth, it is most interesting that, at what could be the end of their lives, so many people with widely varying life experiences focus on the issues of loving and learning.

What higher goals could anyone have than to live as though the two most important things in life are to love and to learn?

If parents would accept that philosophy, we could more easily address the issue of failed relationships. Then we would know that we have done our best if we have loved our child. We have done our best if we have learned from our experience as a parent. *We cannot do better than our best.* Nor are we expected to.

An Exercise for Healing Broken Relationships

Three years ago I attended a conference at which I participated in a lovely guided imagery exercise that was designed to help participants view broken relationships in a new way. Some of the workshop participants used it to work on letting go of a loved one who had died. Others, such as myself, used it to better accept a relationship in which there did not seem to be a possibility of directly resolving differences between us and another person. At that time I didn't know where David was, so this exercise seemed especially appropriate.

Since then I have adapted the exercise in several ways and have used it for a variety of clients. This guided imagery exercise can provide you with insights you had not previously known about another person or about yourself. It can help you discover aspects of the relationship you can change without requiring the other person to change. And it can allow you to become more accepting of the other person in ways that, until now, you have not been able to see. You may want to use this exercise for people other than your adult child, such as an ex-spouse and ex-friends.

If you have not done imagery before, be assured that this process does not "force" you to go someplace in your mind you do not want to go or do something you do not want to do. Everything that happens to you will be what *you* decide and what is best for you to gain from this experience. Imagery exercises are valuable because they make use of the healing metaphors and imagery of the right brain, by-passing the more structured analysis of the left brain that sometimes insists there is only one way to view a situation.

To use the following as a guided imagery exercise, read it slowly into a tape recorder, pausing at the places indicated, or have a friend read it to you. Or you may just want to read it several times (to understand what you are to do) and then complete the exercise without a tape recording.

After you are through, you may want to take a few moments and write about what happened during the exercise. Some people find it helpful to do the exercise more than once.

Let yourself become as comfortable as possible. Allow yourself to be gently supported by the chair or sofa on which you are sitting and move, if you must, to find the most relaxing position. As you let your body find its comfort, allow your eyes to gently close. . .

Now begin to relax by taking a few slow, deep, abdominal breaths, filling your lungs to capacity and releasing the air as completely as possible . . . Each time you breathe out, say to yourself, "I am relaxing. . ." After two or three of these deep breaths, let your body breathe according to its own natural rhythm, slowly and easily . . .

Each time you inhale and exhale normally, allow yourself to become twice as relaxed as you were a moment before . . . Twice as comfortable . . . Twice as peaceful . . . With each breath every cell of your body becomes at ease . . . You find yourself in a state of pleasant, relaxed consciousness . . .

And now imagine that you are standing on a grassy low hill near the sea. You can smell the clean sea air and hear the sounds of birds as they circle overhead and onto the beach below. You notice a path that follows a stream flowing gently into the sea. You take the path and walk slowly to the shore, and then along the shoreline until you come to a dock where a fairly large boat is tied. The weather is perfect and you imagine it would be a good day for taking a boat ride across that sea, or to various places along the sea's edge. Allow yourself to experience being here in a place of calm, serene beauty with a sense of potential healing all around you . . .

As you look back toward the hill on which you were first standing, you notice that there is another path, different from the one you took, that also leads to the shore and then to the dock. You notice on the path a person who, at one time, had been in a relationship with you but with whom you now have a conflict that keeps you physically or emotionally apart. You can see him or her clearly, and even though you may have had difficulty being together in the past, now you realize that no harm will come to either of you in this place.

You watch as the person walks along the path and slowly comes toward you. You greet each other and walk together toward the boat. During this time you discuss how one of you will go on the boat and one of you will wait on the shore. There are a number of reasons why either one of you should go or stay, but you realize that the journey is more necessary for the one than for the other. Perhaps you talk about where it is that either one of you needs to go. You discuss the fact that sometimes people who set out on a voyage and plan to return may discover during their trip that other places hold a strong attraction for them. And so it may be possible that the person taking the trip will not return for some reason.

Once you have decided who will take the journey and who will wait on shore, you pay closer attention to the details of the boat. What does the boat look like? Notice what provisions are already on the boat and which ones still need to be brought on board. How do you feel about the boat and what it has to offer the one who will be traveling? . . .

Now the one who is to take the journey gets on the boat. The one remaining behind unties the rope that holds the boat to the dock and watches as the boat moves slowly away into the distance and out of sight. The person on shore will experience this time in a way that is just right for that person. The journey may last only a short time, or many months or years may be needed before the journey is over. Since this is an experience in the nonlinear part of the mind, time is not of consequence; the journey can last as long as either of you needs for it to last.

Let the journey begin . . .

Now it is almost time for the boat to return to shore. Does the boat return? If it does not, allow the person on shore to accept the choice of the one who does not return. Have the person who has been waiting sit for a while and consider what it means to allow another person to choose his or her own destiny.

If the boat does return, have the person on shore greet the one who has gone on the journey. Find a comfortable place to sit and talk with the other person heart-to-heart about what happened to each of you while you were apart. You may experience this conversation as a real dialogue in which first one of you and then the other speaks. Or you may just get a sense of what happens as you and the other person discuss what you experienced while you were apart . . .

What do you learn that you had not realized before? What happens as you open yourself to listen to what is in the heart of the other? . . .

As you prepare to part, remember that you can return to this place and talk again any time you need to. And now say goodbye and walk back to the hill on separate paths . .

Become aware of the room again and take a deep breath. As you exhale, accept the healing and insights from this experience as being just right for you at this time. And when you feel ready, open your eyes.

Creating a Story of Healing

The stories we tell about our lives are not fixed and immutable, any more than our lives are fixed and immutable. The thousands of circumstances we have experienced over the years provide a wealth of possible meanings and interpretations. No one of them defines the underlying meaning and substance of events in our lives. But we keep repeating that story over and over again until we are convinced it is the *only* interpretation *anyone* could possibly arrive at, if they knew what we know.

If our story is a happy one, we don't have any incentive to change it. This is not the case with the story of disappointed parents who are unable to reconcile with their children. Yet just as we can discover new options by looking through different windows, we can discover that there is more than one story that can reflect what happened between us and our child.

If you are willing to entertain the *possibility* that your experiences need not be viewed as darkly as you have previously viewed them, you might try a story writing exercise I created. As difficult as it may seem to you now, this exercise can transform your story of conflict and pain into one of acceptance and peace.

This exercise will take a fair amount of time to complete; at least weeks, and probably months. It will be time and energy well spent. And while you can begin at any time, it is best if you wait until after you have worked through most of the tasks in the five stages of healing. Then, after those things have not been able to bring your child back to you, telling your story in a different way can describe the broken relationship in more healing terms.

To begin, find a quiet place, perhaps your private retreat, and sit down to consider what stories you tell yourself, and others, about your family's situation. What is the role you have assigned yourself and what is the role you have assigned your child? What emphasis do you give to each part? When you know how you want this tale to be told, begin with "Once upon a time . . ." (or something else if you wish) and write the first draft of the story of your relationship with your child. Be as creative as you can, perhaps telling your story as though it were about someone else. Write it down as thoroughly as possible and then put it aside.

The next time you feel like working on the story, read what you have written so far and notice what it feels like to have your story on paper. Since stories with many-faceted, complex emotions often change from one telling to the next, notice whether you still feel the way you felt when you first wrote it or whether some feelings have shifted. If something you had written now seems unimportant, or if you are ambivalent about some things you had previously held as absolutes, think about how you might change those things in writing the next draft. Leave this draft for your next visit.

When you return, read the story again and think about how you may want to rewrite it. This time make the rewrite shorter, if possible, leaving in only what you know are the important parts and discarding what is not essential.

Repeat this process as many times as you need, making the story more and more brief. You may even try seeing whether you can tell your story in one sentence! Long or short, realize that your story expresses, in a style that is uniquely yours, essential truths of what has happened. Your story is an important version of the unresolvable rift between you and your child, but remember, too, that it is not the absolute, definitive, final word.

When you have finished, notice what changes have happened to your story since you first began telling it. Notice that each retelling contains elements of the truth, with the whole picture evolving as you interpret events in a different way.

Writing a Letter of Closure

Two and a half years ago I met a woman whose son had recently died of cancer. As we talked, she told me that her son, who was the same age as mine, had abused drugs and alcohol before his diagnosis and continued to blame other people whenever he got into trouble. Knowing that her son was dying, she was able to share with him the things she wanted to say. When he died, she felt their relationship was complete.

Our conversation made me realize that if David died, which was surely possible because he was living on the streets at the time, I would not only feel a deep loss, I would also know I had not shared with him all I wanted to share. I decided to write a letter to him, with a personal copy to each of our children. Since I sometimes over-explain myself, the letter was very long (I would write a shorter one if I were doing it today). However, the purpose was to express what I wanted to say. I did. If it took a long time to read, so be it. If my children did not understand what I was trying to say, so be it. I had done my best and felt a real sense of closure in my relationship with David at that time.

Some time later I was talking with him on the phone about another matter and asked him what the letter had meant to him. His only comment was, "It's apparently something you needed to say, and you have a right to your opinion." That's not exactly the reaction I had hoped for, but at least I assumed he had read it. It would have been great if he had said, "Gee, Mom, now that I see how much you love me and how my situation has affected the whole family, I'm going to enter a treatment program and get a job." But that's just wishful thinking. I had no right to expect or demand him to respond in any particular way; nor was that my intent.

Since I wrote that letter, I have helped other parents write to their children. Before writing those letters, however, it has always been essential that the parent be willing to explore honestly *why* she wants to write. Only then can she be assured that the letter will not become a rehash of old fights, a defensive and angry diatribe, or a subtle manipulation to get the child to change. The primary purpose of these letters, after all, is to bring closure to a broken relationship, to acknowledge that, as things now stand, there does not seem to be a possibility for reconciliation, even though that is what the parent would prefer.

The origin of your letter arises out of conflict, of course, and you will want to take plenty of time deciding what should be included and excluded. You don't want to fan the flames but to put them out.

While there are many approaches you can take in writing your letter, I offer the following as important guidelines.

- Say why you are sending a letter at this time. Perhaps you may want to tell your child that after doing some work on your own issues you have decided to put past conflicts behind you by acknowledging those things that are unlikely to change.

- Make certain that the letter is an expression of love.

- Be honest in what you say and in how you say it. And remember that any attempts at manipulation are only likely to drive your child further away.

- Be sure to tell your child that what you write is *your* perspective of what has happened and not necessarily "the truth."

- Assume that your child is in pain over the rift in the family, even though he may *seem* not to care; a cavalier attitude can hide a great deal of pain. Let him know you understand that painful emotions are possibly the reason he has chosen not to be open to reconciliation and that you hope he is able eventually to find peace to heal his own pain.

- Let your child know you recognize that he has a right to make the choices he has made and you also recognize that his choices are reasonable to him, even though you do not understand them.

- Do not accuse him of ruining your life or causing you physical problems. (Although I had a back operation brought on by stress during a time when there was much turmoil over problems with David, I have never blamed him for *my* inability to handle stress more effectively.)

- Acknowledge that you influenced him in many ways when he was a child and accept responsibility for your part in the current problems between you. Do not, however, take all the responsibility in the hope that, by doing so, he will return to the bosom of the family. He is an adult and responsible for his own actions.

- Realize that your spouse or another significant person in your child's life also influenced him, both positively and negatively, and you may want to discuss that person as well. Be careful, however, to acknowledge that your view of that person is your own and may be distorted by your need to see that person in a particular light.

- Let him know what you appreciate about him and how you hold onto the good times you shared. Do not, however, expect that just because your child enjoyed trips to the beach and family vacations that his perception of problems in your family cannot possibly be true.

- Keep the door open for future contact, if you would like that to happen.

A Ritual for Goodbye and Closure

Rituals remind us of our connections with the past and open us to new adventures in the future. They can be significant passages between the different periods of our lives and the different roles we have played. Fortunately, there are rituals you can create for the closure of relationships, when you may need to change from being a parent who has had a relationship with a child to being a parent who no longer has that relationship. These ritual events are not unlike the ritual discussed earlier in which the process of grief is facilitated by releasing lost dreams through writing them on pieces of paper.

The following ritual is designed to encourage closure by celebrating the best of who your child was in the past and/or is now, even though you are not part of her life. This ceremony is especially helpful for relationships irrevocably broken by death. It can be done privately or can include others who have played important roles in your child's life. You may want to do this ritual only once or several times. Experiment to see what works best for you.

On the anniversary of your child's birth, or some other day that was important to both you and your child, set aside time to experience the love you had for her and what you have learned from the life you shared. Go to a place that was special for her, such as the park or the beach. Bring with you several things to help in the ceremony you plan: pictures you want to remember her by, a poem she liked, a copy of her favorite book, or a scarf in a color she loved. Sit down on a blanket or chair and imagine the spirit of your child is there and is receptive to what you say, glad you have taken this time to honor her.

Begin the "ceremony" by telling your child how you have *loved* her and what it is you have *learned*. You may want to read the story you have written and share what has been going on in your life while you have been estranged. Express your love, resentments, regrets, appreciations, dreams, and memories. Let your words reflect the desire that your child have a successful life and find peace for herself, just as you are finding peace for yourself. Remember that when people who have been good friends part company in strong disagreement, the greatest gift of love is when one sincerely wishes the other success. Do not worry if what you say isn't said perfectly. Your child's heart will understand. Your heart will also be listening, and healing.

The following examples offer a few ideas of the kinds of things you may want to say to your child.

- "When you were very small, Sharon, I was sure that what I felt for you was love, but now I realize it was the love of possessing someone who would love me back, because I never felt really loved before. Now I see that what I thought was love may have suffocated you and driven you away. And so my lesson has been that children are not possessions. We must hold them gently and then release them to their own experiences. I let you go and wish you well."

- "Jeremy, I have always loved you and always will, so it has been difficult for me to be separated from you all these years. I regret so terribly much the mistake I made in allowing your stepfather to come between us when I had a chance to make a difference in our relationship. I understand that you are bitter and that you feel it is better if I do not have contact with you. Since I want so much to include you in my life, I am very sad. When I see little children playing in the park, I cannot help but think of Alex and Bruce and wonder how much they have grown. I would like you to know that I now spend a lot of time with my neighbor's little boys, four and six, who love to come and have cookies. And we sometimes play that silly card game of Fish that you liked so much. I let go and hope you do well on your new job."

- "Paul, our relationship was filled with conflict before you committed suicide, and your leaving has made life that much more difficult. We have been filled with anger, pain and guilt. Now I want to heal the rift that stood between us, a rift that may have been part of the reason you decided to take your life. I am deeply sorry you saw no other way out, but I realize you made that choice, I didn't. Since your death I have spent a lot of time not only remembering the love I tried to give you but learning about my role as a parent in your life. I have chosen this special ceremony to share my feelings with you and I believe that you can hear what I want to say—and that both of us can now be at peace."

One Day at a Time

We have all heard the ancient Chinese saying that a journey of a thousand miles begins with the first step. A newer proverb sees progress in a little different way. This wise saying was created by Jeremy, the son of Paula Caplan, author of *Don't Blame Mother*. He noted that, "On a staircase there is only one real step. The rest are there only to help you along the way."

When you are tempted to become discouraged by the distance you have to go in closing a painful part of your life, remind yourself that all you can do is take one step after the other. And then stop every once in a while to look back and see where you have come from.

On the wall of a friend's house is a poster that says, *"You can't change the past, but you can ruin the present by worrying about the future."* Remember that saying when you start fretting about what may happen in the years ahead. Live each day fully in the present, knowing that by doing so you will be better able to handle what tomorrow will bring.

When you bring healing closure to a relationship that seems blocked to reconciliation, new doors may open when you least expect them. And you will be ready for them.

Epilogue

When I decided to write a book for parents who have difficulty letting go of an adult child who marches to a different drummer, I briefly considered writing it strictly from a professional perspective. I could easily conceal my personal story by claiming it happened to a client. The more I thought about it, however, the more I came to believe that I could help parents best by openly discussing my own difficulties in the journey toward letting go with love.

It is my hope that by sharing my story you can see that you, too, can accept your child no matter what he decides to do with his life. There *is* a light at the end of the tunnel. You will see the light growing brighter and brighter as you move from one stage of healing to the next.

Once I decided to include our family's story, I knew that it would not be fair to Dave if he did not have a chance to read what I had written before it was published, including the epilogue written after the chapters were completed. I was open to any suggestions he might make and to the possibility of including his perspective along with mine. After he read the manuscript, I asked him what he thought about it. He replied, "Mom, your view of things is the way you see them. Go ahead and write the book. I think you should do what you want." It wasn't much different from the response he gave to the letter I described in the last chapter, but in any case, I sensed that he felt okay about having my view of our family's story told to strangers.

In the future I would like to talk with him in greater detail about our separate views of his childhood and current lifestyle. Because of the miles that separate us and infrequent opportunities to visit, we have not really sat down for a serious discussion. When others are around, I have sometimes felt he colors his words to fit the audience, perhaps saying things in ways guaranteed to push my buttons, and I'm possibly more defensive than I need to be. We still have a long way to go before we're both really comfortable with each other. I am well aware that just because my pain has been healed to a very large degree and my heart does not feel as broken as it did five or six years ago does not mean we've arrived at a perfect relationship. Nonetheless, I am sure that the future will be better than the past.

A lot has happened in our family since I began the book. For one thing, I've started calling David by the name he likes best, Dave. For another, we've attended a ceremony in which Dave "married' a woman named Cat. I'll explain the quotation marks in a moment.

Dave and Cat met when she was more or less living on the street with her two sons, Ian and Eli, now three and eight. They all came down to visit for one day two years ago. It was the first time in five years that Dave had been home. While I had the impression that Cat might be a positive influence on him, I didn't expect their relationship would really go anywhere. About a year before that time Dave had called to say he planned to marry another woman, or something to that effect, and I had the distinct impression that he considered them a "permanent" couple.

Three weeks after Dave and Cat's visit, however, he sent us an informal Xeroxed invitation to a wedding for his birthday on September 8th. It would obviously be a fairly casual affair, held near a beautiful redwood grove at Patrick's Point State Park on a large rock that juts out over the Pacific Ocean. Used by many couples for their nuptials, the site is named Wedding Rock.

Their wedding would be the first for our children. In the past, as I have mused on what it would be like to be the mother-of-the-groom or -bride, I've sometimes wondered what kind of dress I would be expected to wear. For this event, however, I only needed to worry about whether I should wear tennis shoes or sandals.

Of far greater concern was the fear that I might allow myself to get hooked by something Dave said or did and create a problem for either him or me. I had come a great distance in my journey to healing. I had stopped trying to change him. I had removed lots of Velcro that used to get caught on everything he did. I had let him go with love, in the sense that I accepted his right to live the life he chose.

His one-day visit in August, however, was not as encouraging for our relationship as I had hoped. It was clear that he was not interested at that time, and probably never will be, in creating a life that could offer him more than a level of bare subsistence. The repairs needed to mend the broken fence between him and Rebecca remained unaddressed. Alcohol and drugs were still a problem. He rolled his own tobacco because, so he said, a doctor told him he had a "nicotine deficiency." He and I had several unpleasant conflicts, but we also had two very brief conversations in which I felt the most connected with him that I've felt in years.

So before going to the wedding I went to see my therapist for a booster shot. She had seen me through much of my journey, and I needed her perspective on this new venture. As we talked about some of the things I had worked on years before, it was nice to affirm that I *had* gone through the stages of healing. I just needed to reinforce what I had learned earlier.

As we talked, I came up with an approach to attending the ceremony that would provide me with the greatest amount of comfort. I would observe the wedding activities as though they were a part of a movie that was being filmed!

Living in the Los Angeles area, we often come across scenes being filmed by television and movie crews. We are fascinated with all the equipment and sometimes watch the actors and actresses play part of a scene. On these occasions we are clearly spectators. The director doesn't want or ask our opinion. He is in charge. I decided I could handle Dave's upcoming wedding by experiencing it just as I do the filming of the segment of a sitcom or a drama. He and Cat were in charge. *I would be a spectator!* With that perspective clearly in mind, I felt very prepared for the ceremony.

Tradition suggested that as parents of the groom we were expected to pay for a rehearsal dinner. So we asked Dave to make the arrangements at a local restaurant where we would meet after our long drive north. Although we couldn't have made it in time for the rehearsal, that didn't matter. There wasn't any. That was the first clue that our son's wedding would be out of the ordinary. The second clue was when he announced that they hadn't gotten around to getting a marriage license. Hence the quotation marks around the word "married."

The ceremony the next day was a strange juxtaposition of tradition and free-flowing, hippie-style originality. The wedding party and guests met in the parking lot and we used smoking bundles of sage to cleanse each other's auras. The best man overslept and didn't arrive until after the ceremony was over, but no one seemed to notice, or care. The bride wore a borrowed white dress and the groom wore a suit we bought him in high school. Both were barefoot.

As in traditional weddings, the couple exchanged rings. After they first put them on their fingers and then removed them, Dave threw them into the ocean. "That way," he said, "we will always know where they are." It's a line from the movie *Harold and Maude*, I think. Considering the fact that I was viewing the event like a movie anyway, it seemed appropriate.

The minister, a friend of theirs, was a pleasant man, a talented carver of fine jewelry and small objects. He didn't have a license, but that didn't matter since the wedding was not legal anyway. However, his philosophy leaned to the whimsical and he claimed (though not seriously) that he was a Druid. He forgot to give the homily he had prepared. However, if I remember correctly, he did ask the traditional questions of "Do you take this man . . ." and "Do you take this woman . . ."

After the ceremony itself, while we were still on the rock, the bride had to throw her bouquet twice because the first time Eli caught it. Then Dave removed a garter which she wore and tossed it to a small group of men. Except for the fact that the bride's son caught the bouquet, this was fairly standard wedding fare. But then the couple broke with tradition altogether.

The bride and groom removed their clothes and streaked from Wedding Rock through the woods to a picnic area where the reception was to be held. If I had been sitting demurely in a church at a formal wedding, I might have fainted. Instead, I laughed heartily with thanks for my decision to view the event without a preconception that it should be the kind of ceremony *I* would have planned. And as I've told the story (I have a snapshot to prove they really *did* streak), the reaction of others is that my story tops any other wedding story they have heard.

At the reception, where the couple changed into street clothes, there were more surprises. I won't bother to relate them all here except to say that it was clear Dave has a circle of friends who admire him, and think he is funny, intelligent, and musically talented. The reception's collection of guests seemed a throwback to the sixties, with many of his friends living on the streets or in marginal conditions. But they appeared satisfied, at least outwardly, with their lifestyle choices. As a full-fledged member of the middle class, I certainly don't understand their values. Yet I appreciate their sense of community and their caring for one another.

Incidentally, a number of his friends were amazed that we had come to the wedding. They said their parents had written them off and would never have made the trip.

A minor point of contention has arisen over whether I should view Dave and Cat as "Mr. and Mrs." They see themselves as husband and wife in a common-law marriage, although California does not recognize common-law marriages. I initially stuck to technicalities. I didn't mind their living together. At least Dave was living in a warm trailer and not on the streets. But because I wasn't sure this arrangement would last, I was reluctant to either accept Cat as a "real" daughter-in-law or her sons as my "grandchildren," which Dave wanted me to do.

Time and circumstances have changed my mind. In fact, one of the circumstances is the most significant postscript to this book. Last October Cat had our first grandchild, a boy named Ki Man Harder.

Because she and Dave don't work, the child will receive Aid for Dependent Children, as do Cat's other two children. That is not the dream I had for my grandchildren any more than it was for my children. Nevertheless, I was glad to hold the baby when we went up there over Thanksgiving. It is clear to me that if I let go of my son with love I can more easily love his children; and I'm at a stage in life in which grandchildren are most welcome.

It's not going to be easy, of course, to curb my tongue and refrain from giving advice on child rearing. After all, I come equipped with not only years of professional training but lots of personal experience as well. My hard won lessons on parenting have been used often when clients have solicited my advice on a wide variety of parenting questions. But I doubt Dave and Cat will ask. (Then again, I don't expect any of my other children will solicit my advice on how to raise their children, any more than most adult children are anxious to have grandparents set the rules for The Parenting Game.) I'm determined to keep my opinions to myself.

I would still like Dave to join society in what I would consider a more "normal" fashion. If he does, his road back will not be easy. He has lost a decade in which he could have completed college and graduate school or learned a trade. He could have begun a successful career. And while it is never too late to change, doors to some careers have already been closed. It is not impossible for our son to turn his life around, as many recovering addicts will attest, but it will be difficult and will take determination.

I can only sit back and watch, wondering what will happen next. Last year we bought a camcorder, as we had long planned to do when we finally became grandparents, and took pictures of Ki, Ian, and Eli. Each time we see Dave's family we will take more video shots as a reminder of what his life is like. Many years from now we will have a drawer full of videos. I don't know what they will reveal, but I do know it won't be dull.

Appendix

What I Have Learned in Fifty Years
by Gary Docherty
A Gift to His Adult Children on Christmas 1990

1. People are different
Accept the fact that people are different. Children grow up and develop their own unique personalities. Each has been molded by their particular culture shock. Every Little League player has a different view of the coach. Don't be surprised when people "act that way"; expect that they will act differently. Try hard to avoid assuming that they have the same outlook on life as you do.

2. It's hard to change people
People resist change. They may change by following someone's example, or by seeing some great benefit to their lifestyle. Don't count on them to change.

3. Don't tell people "don't worry."
Worry is natural. Saying "don't worry" seldom helps. Suggest positive action on something within their control.

4. I am not responsible for my adult children.
Does that sound harsh? Think about it some more. If you keep assuming other adult's responsibilities, it's likely they will not take charge of their own lives. Give your adult children love, help, compassion, sympathy, empathy, and explicit knowledge that you are not assuming their responsibilities.

5. Try new things.
It is easy to get into a rut. Most of us are somewhat fearful of new and different ideas. Overcome fear by discovering your preferred way to explore the unknown: Go it alone, go with your best friend, or go with a group.

6. Never stop learning.

A good student has few preconceived ideas, asks good questions, and reaches good conclusions. This is harder than just plain trying new things, but is more rewarding.

7. Pull the weeds.

Trying too many things can get you into a different rut. Trim your activities to a comfortable range to foster strong growth. Finish what you start.

8. Find your niche.

A popular theory for the nineties is that business will be good in narrowly defined sectors (niches) of the economy. Each person also can find a niche that will put their talents to use in a fulfilling way. What are your talents?

9. See and smell the roses.

One day I realized that I had weeded MJD's rose garden so many times that I hardly noticed the roses. Crawling through the bushes on my hands and knees, pulling up each individual weed in my usual style, I broke off a branch. It was a beautiful rose. It took only a minute or so to see that rose, smell that rose, stand up and look at the whole garden, and then get back to work with a new view point. Use little chunks of time to help you keep the daily details in perspective. It only takes a short time to give the child a "swing swung" before they get bored with that. One minute of sock-pulling with the dog is plenty. Thirty seconds of petting is about all the typical cat will permit. Ten seconds every day for giving your spouse a welcome-home kiss is loving, and wise, time-management.

10. Results are what count.

I used to think that everything had to be done very well (perfect?). The major problem with that idea was that I did not have enough time to do everything very well. The inevitable result was a continuous trail of unfinished projects. I have finally concluded that it's OK to do most things reasonably well, and that's good enough. Getting a "passable" product and "closure" on a project allow me to concentrate on the next project in the pipeline.

Now don't get the idea that I am excusing sloppy work. What is "passable" has to consider the use of final results. Sometimes it is worth investing another ten seconds, maybe even another ten minutes, to get results that count.

Index